GARDENS OF SRI LANKA

Klaus Holzhausen Senake Bandaranayake Shanti Jayawardene

GARDENS OF SRI LANKA

2,000 YEARS OF GARDEN AND LANDSCAPE DESIGN TRADITION

SilvanaEditoriale

Preface

Garden design and landscape architecture are a Sri Lankan legacy that together embody a distinctive aspect of Sinhalese culture. They reflect an understanding of the values and aesthetic qualities of nature throughout a civilization which has survived from pre-Christian times to the present, representing a period of more than twenty-five centuries.

The idea to publish a systematic record of the Sri Lankan heritage of garden and landscape design was initiated by the late Professor Senake Bandaranayake in partnership with the Swiss landscape architect Klaus Holzhausen. After Bandaranayake's death in 2015, the project has been continued, developed and completed by Holzhausen with great enthusiasm and determination.

The tropical climate fostered a traditional domestic architecture which permitted people to live around their houses instead of being confined within them. Larger buildings had generous courtyards with layered greenery allowing the outside to be integrated with the architectural elements. Large verandas became a typical element of Sri Lankan dwellings. The practice identified today as 'landscape architecture' (the discipline has only existed officially in Sri Lanka since the 20th century) has never been limited to gardens. It corresponds to an overall creation that seamlessly intertwined nature with manmade elements. The creative process implies the meticulous selection and understanding of a site in order to integrate the natural elements into the built environment. Many examples of this practice can be found throughout the course of our history. These creations can be identified as landscape-driven architecture instead of the usual architecture-driven landscape.

There are three ways that lead to the understanding of the philosophy of landscape design in Sri Lanka. The first is based on documented information found in chronicles such as the Mahamsa or Culavamsa, which details events and achievements throughout the historical journey of our civilisation. The second approach involves examining the archaeological and architectural remains that are dispersed over the island and are in a decent state of preservation. The third way is the study of the surviving landscape traditions still present in the country. To achieve a comprehensive understanding of the philosophy and tenets of garden history and landscape architecture in Sri Lanka it is important to explore all three of these approaches.

The garden landscapes in Sri Lanka can be categorised as monastic, secular and domestic.

The surrounding landscapes of monastic gardens were not intended to meet aesthetic and beauty principles, but created to provide a peaceful environment necessary for the concentration of the mind during meditation. In order to create an ideal manmade topography for monks living in isolation, Buddhist monasteries have integrated trees, small forests, rocks, boulders, natural streams (following waterways with vavas or large reservoirs), ponds, pathways, natural and artificial caves and other buildings into the design of their gardens. In the so-called double-platform-type meditation monasteries (padhanagara), the platforms were surrounded by water canals with the two platforms joined by a bridge built of massive stone slabs. Ritigala, Arankäle and Manakanda are some of the landscaped Buddhist monasteries built during the 6th and 7th centuries. In the Pabbatha-Vihara-type monasteries the entire building complex was encircled by a broad rectangular water canal. Every monastery was constructed of exquisitely cut stones and featured both large and small ponds storing water for drinking and bathing. The Vessagiriya – Isurumuniya monasteries in Anuradhapura were redesigned in the 5th century under King Kashyapa who built Sigiriya. It is a fascinating creation in a setting with large boulders and caverns. The architectural language found in Vessagiriya, Sigiriya and the Royal Palace Garden of Ranmasu Uyana suggests that the same architect of King Kashyapa may well have been responsible for all of them.

Examples of secular landscape gardens can be found in planned cities like Sigiriya in the 5th century, Polonnaruwa in the 12th century and Kandy in the 18th century. Pleasure gardens and royal palace gardens such as Ranmasu Uyana in Anuradhapura and Sigiriya, Dipauyana in Polonnaruwa, and the case of Kandy provide useful evidence for understanding the spirit of the ancient gardens in Sri Lanka.

Another relevant typology is the domestic forest garden – which masterfully blends art (design) and nature – still popular in hilly country regions.

The present publication does not forget the British Colonial influence, the introduction of home gardens with lawns and flower beds as well as the creation of botanical gardens combining beauty with the conservation of plant species. Moreover, it further draws the reader's attention to the creation of modern gardens by designers of the recent past.

Gardens of Sri Lanka provides a fascinating and insightful inquiry into the accomplishments of twenty-five centuries of gardening tradition that symbolises both the history of Sri Lanka and of humankind in general.

Nimal De Silva

Honorary President/National Trust – Sri Lanka

Foreword

Down to the present day, the general history of gardens has been conceived and determined from a one-sided perspective. Although the garden represents, as we know, a global reality, its representation and theorization have been marked by the model that Europe has, until very recently, imposed on a planetary scale. Starting here, the history of gardens has developed an exemplary diachronic itinerary, from the *kepos* of ancient Greece to the representative gardens of imperial Rome, and continuing with the medieval monastic garden, the great estates of the Renaissance and Baroque periods, and so on up to our days. This primacy of the Eurocentric perspective – which has always implied a blindness to those parts of the world where gardens have developed *differently* – has also imposed a pseudo-universal aesthetic vocabulary over the centuries which excludes anything that does not bend to the diktat of categories such as the classical and the neoclassical, the formal or geometric, the picturesque or irregular, and even to the postmodern conceived as the universal receptacle of all the world's styles inscribed in the great logocentric book of the world's gardens.

While we are aware that this one-sided path does not correspond to the facts on the ground – the aristocratic gardens of ancient Rome are unthinkable without the prior encounter, in the Hellenistic era, with the art of Persian gardens; the picturesque or irregular gardens of the 18th century depend to such an extent on contact with Asia, that they were initially simply referred to as Anglo-Chinese gardens – the mainstream of garden aesthetics and historiography continues to follow the so-called 'Western' model.

Back when Michel Foucault first coined the term 'heterotopia' applied to gardens, we should already have begun to take an interest in an otherness that is not just that of the individual garden, but of other traditions and types of garden excluded from the dominant *catalogue raisonné*. However, even a superficial and unscientific interest in the gardens of Sri Lanka is enough to reveal that – and this comes as a major shock – gardens there have for many centuries had possibilities that we have not wanted to see. In the light of what there is, quite simply, to discover on this island, which could well be called 'the island of gardens', it seems at first sight inexplicable that we have had to wait until now to contemplate and celebrate the publication of a book dedicated solely to the gardens of Sri Lanka. It was Senake Bandaranayake (1938-2015), since his excavation experience in Sigiriya probably one of the very first real garden archaeologists worldwide, who identified in the ancient Sri Lankan civilisation a 'pure garden form'. His was the idea too to dedicate an entire study to the gardens of Sri Lanka.

Following the amazing journey proposed by Klaus Holzhausen and the authors of this volume, one goes from surprise to surprise. First of all, there's the unsuspected world of the great royal estates. While transposing us to a distant time, these compositions, which combine a certain archaism with the technical exuberance of the art of water control, strike us with their sublime dimension. Spatial generosity here reflects a local aristocratic civilization which found in the garden the highest point of its art. Another essential tradition presented in this volume is that of Sri Lanka's monastic gardens. The sheer number of Buddhist monasteries scattered all over the island since almost 2,000 years is incredible. Most of these sites contain rather gardens than buildings. Designed for the meditative practice of monks, they surprise by their exquisite sobriety and sophisticated geometry. Monastic gardens and royal gardens stimulated each-other during the centuries.

Then there's the more complex case of colonial gardens, those magical but often forced amalgams between a self-celebrating culture from outside and the local topography and vegetation. Like the country's history, these achievements are both colonial wounds and living idylls; they are the painful but telling result of compromise and violence, but also forms of landscape beauty born of the very contradictions that shaped them.

Last but not least – and the volume that Klaus Holzhausen, as a true prophet of the places he has traversed for nearly three decades, makes clear – is the existence of contemporary gardens that have, physically and immediately for those lucky enough to walk through them, an extraordinary force and something to teach the world. In the field of garden design, the question of what is 'modern' is controversial, to the point where some even claim that there has never been anything such as a modern revolution in garden history. Maybe the garden took a leap forward without ever being modern in order to become immediately 'postmodern', that is a garden of gardens of gardens... Sri Lanka's contemporary gardens seem however to have squared the circle by combining a modern language (marked by the idea of reduction, by the free play of forms, by a break with the sheer exuberance of vegetation) with a centuries-old tradition of spatial generosity, and an unusual sensibility for the individual spirit of the place. A garden like Lunuganga, Geoffrey Bawa's magnificent work of total art, illustrates the successful synthesis between the art of gardens from different periods and horizons and the young discipline of landscape architecture. Extreme simplicity, even in the use of colors, and the idea of palimpsest, the ability to cite examples from the past, have enabled here a perfect fusion.

A book on gardens is always partly frustrating, since what we would like to do is to stroll in the magical spaces described. The extremely meticulous way in which *Gardens of Sri Lanka* has been elaborated and the quality of the iconic and written documentation permit readers however to already be *there* and to discover page after page the existence of another world.

Michael Jakob

Genesis of the Book and Acknowledgements

It all started with my first trips to Sri Lanka at the end of the 1990s where, as a landscape architect, I was surprised and impressed by the country's wonderful gardens, both ancient and modern. Later, through research, I learned that the archaeologist and art historian, Professor Senake Bandaranayake, had led the garden excavations in Sigiriya and elsewhere. I then contacted Senake in 2005 in the hopes of corresponding with him. He immediately agreed to receive me in his office at the Postgraduate Institute of Archeology (PGIAR) in Colombo.

After a long conversation, I understood his deep interest and knowledge of the ancient and modern gardens of Sri Lanka. Finally, he told me that he was thinking about writing a book on the history of Sri Lankan gardens. But dealing fully with such a subject would benefit from the combined contributions of an archeologist such as himself, and the sensitivity and experience of a landscape architect. Accordingly, he invited me to collaborate on this book, an invitation that I accepted without hesitation. It was the beginning of a very rewarding friendship.

In 2006, we defined the structure of the book and developed a table of contents. We agreed on a division of labor: Senake was to write the texts, while I was to survey and photograph all the sites that were to be featured in the book, as well as drawing up the plans. It was in February 2008 that I began my systematic campaign of photography and surveying. This lasted until 2013-2014, and even beyond.

Very soon after starting working on the book, we understood that aerial photos of certain important sites would be very useful for the reader. A sponsor was ready to finance the rental of a helicopter. So, in February 2010, my friend Olivier Lasserre – a Swiss landscape architect and experienced aerial photographer – and I rented a helicopter from the Sri Lankan army for four days. We took as many photos as possible in six flights over Sigiriya – Kandalama, Polonnaruwa, Anuradhapura and Mihintale.

2011, Senake became ill, but finishing the book was for him an essential and heartfelt project. We met each other several times every year and exchanged e-mails up until his last day.

In 2012, Senake asked the historian of architecture Shanti Jayawardene, to write the chapter on 'Monastic Gardens' as well as the introduction to the chapter on 'Colonial Encounter'. She accepted this task with enthusiasm.

During Senake's long illness, his wife Manel Fonseka was of precious help to him. Thanks to her, he was able to complete the Royal Gardens chapter. After he passed away in 2015, we were faced with the question of how to proceed.

With Manel's agreement, I 'inherited' this book project, which I needed to finish. In a quite natural way, Shanti Jayawardene became my Sri Lankan partner. She continued to write the texts she took over and was of great help.

Because of the illness and death of my wife Sylvia in 2016, progress on the book stopped until 2018.

Another important source of help during these last year's came from my friend in Geneva, Professor Michael Jakob, a landscape historian. With their great experience in editing books, he and his wife Maura took over much of the task of editing the work.

For the computer processing of all plans and drawings, and for some translations, a Franco-American architect in Lausanne, Charlotte Thietart, was ready to help me.

And last but not least, the creation and production of such a book requires financing. Fortunately, my

Swiss-American friend and colleague, Gianni Biaggi de Blasys, who travelled with me two times to Sri Lanka, was ready to be our main sponsor. Other Swiss landscape architects joined us. So, I can now state with confidence that the conception and development of this book was a truly Sri Lankan-Swiss collaboration!

I wish to thank all those who shared their time and experience with me and who have so generously contributed to this endeavour. As well as to the people mentioned above, I would like to express my gratitude to my other Sri Lankan and Swiss friends: Nimal De Silva for authorizing our helicopter flights over the Cultural Triangle sites and for his 'Foreword'; the architects Jayatissa Herath for locating the archaeological documents I needed at the PGIAR library and Ajantha Ranaweera for the map of Sri Lanka and for accompanying me to the Western Monasteries; the archaeologist Kusumsiri Kodithuwakku for guiding me through some of the old monasteries in the Dambulla region; Upali Siriwardena, who for more than twenty years was my driver and guide in many difficult-to-find places and who resolved all of our logistical problems with aptitude and reliability; and Ivan Baranowski in Zurich for the miraculous photo-editing and composing he undertook for me.

Finally, my warmest thoughts return to those who are no longer with us: to those who will never be able to enjoy this book, to which they contributed so much – to Senake Bandaranayake; to Olivier Lasserre; to Laki Senanayake; and to my beloved partner Sylvia Krenz, who accompanied me on this adventure.

Klaus Holzhausen

Contents

The 5th-century Sigiriya complex is the best-known example of royal gardens in Sri Lanka, with the palace garden at the top of the rock and the water garden in the plain. View from the north-east.

General Introduction

Prof. Senake Bandaranayake

It is a paradox underlying the complex histories of gardens[1] in Asia that some are extremely well known and synonymous with the notion of the ideal garden, while others are still unknown, unrecognised, or unrecorded. One of the earliest expressions of garden art in the world are the vestigial remains of the 6th-century BCE Persian gardens at Pasargad in Iran, the capital of Cyrus the Great. Persian, Chinese, Japanese and Mughal gardens are familiar subjects of art-historical discourse. Little is known or said, however, about the earliest gardens in China, such as the royal garden of the Southern Yue State in Guangzhou (circa 204-111 BCE), or the stone arrangements at Iga-Kambe, in the Western Mie Prefecture, the site of an old royal palace in Japan, dating from the 4th century CE. At the other end of the time scale, known but not much talked about, we find one of the largest garden complexes in Asia, the 18th- and 19th-century Chinese Yuanming Yuan, the Garden of Perfect Brightness, a combination of three earlier gardens.[2]

These landmarks of Asian garden history extend over a period of more than two millennia. During this long period the garden traditions of Sri Lanka display an important continuity which stretches, with obvious discontinuities, from proto-historic times to the present day. The rich history of Sri Lankan gardens extends, we might say, from the boulder-and-terrace gardens of the rock-shelter Buddhist monasteries at Dambulla, founded between the 3rd and 1st centuries BCE, to the designed landscape of the 17th to 19th centuries in the royal city of Kandy – both World Heritage sites – and to contemporary examples of outstanding merit, such as Lunuganga or the Boulder Garden Hotel.

The garden traditions of South Asia are evidenced in literature from very early times, most particularly in Buddhist texts and histories and also in Vedic and

The same Sigiriya royal garden seen from the west with the rock in the centre and its east-west main axis through the water garden.

classical Sanskrit sources from as far back as the first millennium BCE, or earlier. They indicate three basic contexts in which the concept of the garden arose:

- first, the urban or suburban park or forest grove in which kings, nobles, merchants, travellers, religious teachers and monks took refuge from the heat and dust, noise and fervid activity of urban conditions;
- secondly, the distant forest, cave or mountain retreat of ascetics and sages who favoured isolation and quietude away from human settlement;
- thirdly, the water festivals and water sports associated with many urban and rural cultures, and with royal courts. In this literature, forests, groves, and parks,[3] trees and flowers, and water bodies provide a base for the evocation and celebration of the richness of nature, its beauty, symbolism, fertility, and restorative powers, for the 'culture of flowers', and the pleasure of the development of culture in the context of gardens.

The descriptions of royal, public, and domestic gardens indicate that they were essential elements in city planning, as well as pointers to aesthetic sensitivity, wealth, social status, territoriality, and political power, and that they were also implicit or explicit expressions of philosophies of nature. In later years, the Mughal and other princely gardens of India and Pakistan, many of them relatively well preserved, are extensively documented in textual records, and contemporary miniature paintings which evoke, in a most expressive way, the courtly functions and culture of leisure associated with them. However, the only example of a royal garden from an earlier period in a fair state of archaeological preservation is the one in Sigiriya.

Written sources and archaeological approach

Sri Lanka takes its place in Asian garden history not only by virtue of its chronicle accounts, inscriptional records and literary descriptions of gardens and natural environments, but even more so on account of the unique survival of the archaeological remains of many planned garden forms, especially from time horizons earlier than those of surviving historic gardens in other South Asian societies and cultures. The Sri Lankan relict gardens are an archaeological phenomenon little seen elsewhere in Asia from a period prior to the 13th century.

Typical rock shelters of early monastic settlements under natural boulders at Vessagiriya near Anuradhapura. A basic element is the drip ledge, cut into the rock, which prevents rainwater from running behind. Often the front of the shelter was closed by a wall.

Sri Lankan chronicles, maintained in contemporary or near contemporary court and monastic records and oral traditions, were first written down in narrative form between the 3rd and 6th centuries CE and periodically updated. They echo Buddhist canonical literature in referring to royal and suburban public parks and groves donated by the first Buddhist kings as sites for the early monasteries. This is confirmed by the archaeological evidence which shows the city of Anuradhapura surrounded by a landscape of well-planned monastic complexes of great antiquity, in which parkland, trees, axial avenues, spatial 'compartments' and static and moving water bodies played a prominent and vital role. The close relationship between parks, gardens and water bodies, and the origins of the Sri Lankan Buddhist monastery is well reflected in the chronicle description of the founding of the Mahavihara, the central monastery at Anuradhapura, in the mid-3rd century BCE by the Arahat Mahinda. Even in translation from the original Pali verse to English prose the gentle, matter-of-fact poetry of the narrative, though succint, is evocative of the atmosphere of its setting:

> [...] the people who had assembled there [...] prepared seats for the *theras* outside the southern gate, in the pleasant Nandana-garden in the royal park, thickly shaded, cool, and covered with verdure. The *thera* [Mahinda] went forth by the south gate and seated himself there [...] So, there in the grove, evening fell. Then the *theras* set forth saying: 'We will go hence to the mountain.' [...] Approaching the *thera* [Mahinda] [...][the king] said to him: 'It is evening-time and the mountain is far away; but here in the Nandana-garden is a pleasant place to rest.' When they answered: 'It is not fitting (for us) being too near the city,' [the king said]: 'The Mahamegha-park is neither too far nor too near; pleasant [is it] and water and shade abound there; may it please you to rest there.' (*Mv* 15.1-10).[4]

We may compare this with a rare, realistic image of city life extracted from a later part of the chronicle describing the urban environment from which the monks were seeking to distance themselves:

> [...] in this beautiful town [...] different kinds of streets [were] laid down [...] with many thousands of dwellings of two, three and more storeys [...] with various bazaars where all wares were to be had and in which day by day there was incessant traffic of elephants, horses, and chariots [...] here and there enlivened by people who were ever indulging in great games. (*Mv* 73.148-150).

The early monastic settlements developed over time into well-planned urban, suburban, and rural monasteries (ârâma or *vihara*), whose principal elements were repeated through the centuries with many changes and variations of form and character. The same traditional ancestry as that of the park or grove monastery applies to the alternative monastery type, the *giri vihâra* or 'mountain monastery'. In these cases, a rocky, boulder-strewn mountain peak or more often a hillside slope was selected, and rock shelters fashioned from the rock-face or from massive boulders. The boulders themselves were preserved in their natural form, but often had a hall or pavilion erected on their summits, and lean-to roofs around their bases, creating a distinctive rock-associated architecture. These boulder gardens also incorporate another garden form, the terrace garden, in which the boulder-strewn slopes of a mountain are arranged in a series of successive terraces. Vestigial remains of such boulder-and-terrace garden complexes appear in the Sri Lankan archaeological record at hundreds of sites with inscriptions dating from the 3rd century BCE to the 1st century CE and later. These boulder-and-terrace gardens continue to be used – or renewed from time to time – throughout the centuries. They are a particular Sri Lankan contribution to garden history.[5]

This octagonal pool against a huge boulder at Sigiriya marks the end of the water garden and the beginning of the boulder garden.

The vocabulary of Sri Lankan garden design

Many elements of Sri Lankan garden design in royal and monastic contexts recur throughout the centuries. We see the importance attached to natural site topography and scenic landscape views, to specific forms of architecture and garden space, to the juxtaposition of natural boulders and geometrically oriented water bodies and to the frequent use of water palaces and stone-lined pools. Varying levels of terracing, the inspired combination of symmetry and asymmetry, and axial and radial planning are other main features of these gardens.

Furthermore, we encounter everywhere the important role of water, and of water rituals, some probably pre-Buddhist in origin. The ritual association with water and the construction of pools and gardens, appears throughout the chronicle as an important symbolic action connected with kingship.[6] This is clearly illustrated in the actions of the first two founder-kings of Anuradhapura, the semi-historical Pandukabhaya, (the 'grandson of a lion') and his son Mutasiva. Pandukabhaya had 'solemnized his own consecration' (*Mv* 10.78) with water from a sacred and historic natural pond which 'he had deepened and abundantly filled with water' (*Mv* 10.78, 83). The pond was renamed Jayavapi, the Lake of Victory.[7] An even more elaborate gesture is that of King Mutasiva, whose first action after his consecration was the setting out of the beautiful Mahameghavana garden (the 'Garden of the Great Rain-Cloud'), rich in all the excellent qualities which its name promises and provided with both fruit trees and flowering trees (*Mv* 11-12).

Water resources were crucial to the developing Anuradhapura civilization. It was not only water's utilitarian factor that is its function in all human settlements, but also that it is the principal element in an economic structure in which trade and craft production also played a major role. It was water, we might say, that supported the culture of gardens: water management as both the source and the product of an advanced technology of irrigation, and water gardens as a medium of expression for the elaborate aesthetics of Sri Lankan garden art.

Water sports are an obvious correlative of these intricate water gardens. In the Late Historical Period, from the 13th century onwards, the description of royal water sports becomes a standard feature of epic and courtly poetry. While the general opinion is that these descriptions are literary constructs derived from Sanskrit poetry, the vigorous energy of the Sri Lankan texts, complemented by archaeological remains suggests – at least in an number of contexts – a closer proximity to reality than to classical literature.[8] Two verses presenting an eye-witness account of popular water games in the Kelani River in a poem, the *Hamsa-sandesaya,* by an unknown 15th century poet illustrate the point well:

> Men who know the ways of whirlpools and currents
> jump from the banks, plunge into deep water
> vanish under the flood, strike out into the distance
> come to the surface splashing and playing their water games
>
> The women float in the river turning on their backs
> like the charm of a long garden pool with faces like lotuses
> dark lily eyes, swan bosoms, eyebrows and eye lashes dark
> like glistening swarms of bees gambolling to their hearts' content.[9]

Writing in the archaeological context of the royal garden, the Goldfish Park in Anuradhapura, Senarat Paranavitana presents a list of special garden features drawn from Sanskrit and Pali, literary sources, including the Buddhist birth stories (the *Jatakas*), classical Sanskrit dramas and *silpasastras* (technical handbooks), pre-eminently the *Upavanavinoda*, as well as a Sanskrit manual on horticulture and the management and maintenance of gardens.[10] Paranavitana is one of the founding fathers of Sri Lankan archaeology, who, in the 1940s, initiated garden archaeology in Sri Lanka in his excavations at the Gold Fish Park in Anuradhapura and the water gardens at Sigiriya. Thanks to Paranavitana's observations we learn about a number of special features which in addition to avenues of flowering trees and shrubs and creepers helped to beautify parks in ancient India. Among them are bathing ponds whose banks were lined with carved stones, ponds in which were grown various aquatic flowers, artificial sheets of water, artificial peaks and caves, bowers formed of flowering creepers such as Jasmin, shower-bath houses, bath houses with douches, bowers formed of plantain trees, houses with swings, picture-galleries, and stone seats.[11] Even if these elements come mainly from Indian literary sources, the available technology and style apply to the entire region, classic Indian models having enriched and inspired local practice in a wide area of South-East Asia.

The *pure* garden form

The most remarkable garden remains in Sri Lanka are the examples of what we might call the 'pure' garden form. What is meant by this – the term is somewhat imprecise but difficult to replace with any other – is a garden with an autonomous or semi-autonomous existence, independent of a building complex, or, as in the case of a courtyard within a building, a clearly demarcated but substantial part of a larger architectural whole. The pure form is best represented by the gardens at

The north-western part of the man-made Parakrama lake at Polonnaruwa showing the 'Garden of Islands' (or Dipa-uyana). Two islands are visible, the third one is further away on the left.

Sigiriya and the Ranmasu Uyana (or Royal Goldfish Park) in Anuradhapura. A rare example of a monastic garden that may also be included in this category is the miniature lake-garden and adjoining boulder-and-terrace garden complex of the Kaludiya Pokuna monastery at Mihintale.

Despite its being a World Heritage Site, it is not widely known that the 5th century palace, garden and monastery complex at Sigiriya is one of the world's earliest surviving large-scale gardens whose overall layout and most significant features are still in a fair state of archaeological preservation. The great significance of the Sigiriya gardens to Sri Lankan and world garden history lies in two factors: their antiquity and the degree of preservation of the original 5th century conception. Sigiriya is the result of an ingenious combination, on a grand scale, with three distinctively different, but intermingled modes of garden design: boulder gardens, terrace gardens, and water gardens, representing almost the entire range of the vocabulary of Sri Lankan garden design.

Elsewhere in Sri Lanka several monastic sites exist where the garden, now only visible in a skeletal form, is an integral part of a manmade landscape, a setting for the monastic buildings – frequently of startling originality, as in the rock-based meditation monasteries in the once forested western outskirts of Anuradhapura, or at hillside sites such as Ritigala and Nuvaragalkanda.

Secular gardens in this category – where the garden form is integrated into the overall architectural layout – can be seen in two vestigial gardens in the 12th century royal precincts at Polonnaruwa. The more substantial of these is the 'Island Park' or Dipauyana ('Dipa-uyana'), which contains the archaeological remains of three islands, water palaces, at least one of them relatively well-preserved, and parts of an elaborate royal

A typical landmark stupa on the highest point of a mountain, shown here at Mihintale.

At Sigiriya the western length of the inner moat is dramatically aligned with the perfectly conical peak of the Nuvaragalkanda range lying exactly to the south.

bath, all associated with a colossal man-made lake, the Sea of Parakrama.

As in Anuradhapura, the Buddhist monasteries of Polonnaruwa display the subtle combination of site selection, level changes, monumental and ancillary buildings, open garden spaces, and hydraulics, all regular features of Sri Lankan architectural planning. They are well described in a classic text by Senarat Paranavitana dealing with the Alahana Parivena complex, one of the major monasteries in Polonnaruwa:

> The architects of old have given as much consideration to the aesthetic effects created by a whole ensemble of related buildings as they have to the design of an individual edifice [...] The skill with which the elevation of the ground had been made use of in order to locate on it the principal edifices intended for religious worship or ecclesiastical purposes – the image-house, the *stupa*, and the chapter house. The sloping ground on all sides of this central eminence has been made into terraces, and on them were located the *stupas* of lesser importance, the residential quarters for the monks, their refectories, libraries and other adjuncts, necessary for the life of a highly organized religious fraternity [...] Ponds and sheets of water reflected the forms of the main buildings and the flowering trees which were planted at intervals must have contributed to the serenity of the scene. Natural boulders were made to harmonise with the scheme of building and the various edifices no doubt sat easily in their surroundings.[12]

In his pioneering excavations of the Sigiriya Water Gardens in the 1950s, Paranavitana was also the first to observe the combination of symmetry and asymmetry as a distinctive feature of Sri Lankan garden design. The masters of garden design generally worked on a broad canvas. Their designed landscapes were often based on an ambitious programme, visible immediately even to the casual observer at sites such as Anuradhapura, Mihintale, Sigiriya, Ritigala, Kandy and the Giri monasteries like Dambulla, Varana, Situlpahuva and several other similar locations throughout the country.

Sigiriya once again occupies a special place in the context of landscape design. The palace site on the summit of the rock offers extraordinary vistas. Forming the centre point of the axial median running through the middle of the water gardens, on the west, and the inner and outer cities, on the east, it provides a near 360-degree view of a horizon rim of distant mountains. A recent discovery in the Sigiriya basin and beyond is an ancient practice of building a small but (originally) highly visible stupa on the highest point of each mountain pressing the entire landscape into a cultural statement. The stupas were not always easily accessible and were essentially symbolic markers rather than votive monuments.

A related phenomenon is that of 'borrowed landscape' – a familiar feature in Japanese gardens and known as *shakkei* – where distant landscape elements outside a garden are brought into the garden as a part of a visual composition. Extraordinarily dramatic examples of this are to be seen at the south-western corner of the Inner Moat at Sigiriya and in the interconnected views at the Kaludiya Pokuna complex at Mihintale and its mountain backdrop. At Sigiriya the western length of the moat is dramatically aligned with the perfectly conical peak of the Nuvaragalkanda range lying directly to the south. At Mihintale the three mountain peaks of Anaïkuttikanda, Atveherakanda and Rajgirilenkanda are visually linked with each other and with Kaludiya Pokuna.

The planners of Sigiriya, as at many other similar sites in Sri Lanka, underline their passionate involvement with landscape at almost every location of some importance. Time and time again when visiting a historic site, one is struck by the way in which site selection is in harmony with the vista, the scenic view, the horizon. Viewed from different points in the Hantana range, the city and lake at Kandy look like a gem set in a piece of jewellery, while the forested mountain slopes of Udavattakale and Hantana form a landscape backdrop to the lake, the palace and the Tooth Relic temple.

Literary records and *materia medica* throughout the entire historical period up to the 17th and 18th century are replete with references to varieties of trees, shrubs and flowers. They provide an extensive enumeration of the historical and ornamental vegetation of royal and monastic parks and gardens but little indication of planting design. It is only at the royal garden site at

Sigiriya that excavations have revealed the existence of flower beds and the ubiquitous use of potted plants in palace buildings and gardens. The near contemporary 13th century description of the Nandana Uyana in Polonnaruwa is a rare record of a royal garden in South Asia from such an early period, even though it may contain some descriptive elements derived from texts that are even earlier.

Underpinning both courtly and monastic landscapes is the long tradition of hydraulic engineering, and design knowledge, and land management skills of the elites. To this pool we can add the expertise, knowledge, and labour power of large numbers of people who cut trees, dug the land, built terraces, canals, lakes, walls and monuments and nurtured seedlings, planted trees and flowers and cared for them. We may assume that royal and monastery gardens maintained a very large range of staff on their payroll for performing such tasks. A 10th-century inscription of Mahinda IV (956-972) at Vessagiriya, the southernmost section of the garden complex of which the Goldfish Park is part, gives us a rare insight into the intricate water management system linking the greater irrigation system of the city of Anuradhapura with reservoirs, monastic lands and royal parks on its periphery and the high level of administrative management involved:

> [His] Majesty having thus heard of the dispute [...] gave orders to set up this slab edict in order that lords of royal blood who are officials of royal parks shall, without transgression, observe these [following] regulations. The fields around the vihara...cultivated by means of this water from the Tissawava shall be supplied with water [from the same source] through the medium of a distributing tank, [the flow of water being continued] without interruption, until the top of the aqueduct stone pillar] set up in front of the Moholnanga royal sluice at [a depth of] 4 cubits of water, appears [above water] [...] The water thus set flowing shall be directed to the above-mentioned fields around the monastery, as well as to the gold-fish park, to the nursery, to the pond in the park, and to the lotus pond [...].[13]

Post-classic continuities

The classic garden and landscape traditions of the Early and Middle Historical periods continue in a modified form in the transitions and transformations that mark the Late Historical Period (13th to 19th century). No grand royal or monastery complexes comparable with those of Anuradhapura, Sigiriya or Polonnaruwa were built during this period, although in the 15th and 16th century the royal capital of Kotte was a fortified city larger than Polonnaruwa in the area bounded by its outer ramparts. This lack of monumentality and large-scale complexes was especially applicable to construction in the permanent materials of brick and stone, so that the archaeological readings of the garden traditions of this era are more elusive. Although there are royal and urban complexes with scanty remains at the capital cities of Dambadeniya and Yapahuva (13th century), Kurunegala (14th century), Kotte and Rayigama (16th century), they display shadows of the classic tradition in site selection, urban planning and the use of water. Despite a rich literature of poetry and prose extolling landscape and describing gardens in courtly contexts, archaeology has still to discover substantial remains of royal or elite garden complexes of this period. It is only in the 18th and 19th centuries that we begin to encounter once again a significantly visible continuation of the Sri Lankan garden tradition in Kandy, the last, mountain capital of the Sri Lankan kings, with manorial and monastic courtyard gardens in the Kandyan kingdom, and precinct, terrace and boulder gardens in the southern, western and northern maritime regions.

However, despite the colonial intervention, these areas also contain significant exceptions to a hiatus in garden remains in the Late Historical Period (i.e., 13th-early19th century). This applies especially to the boulder-and-terrace garden complexes that had a continuous or near continuous history, not only in the Kandyan kingdom but also in the southern and western regions of the country, which came under colonial occupation from about the late 16th century onwards. Sites such as Dambulla in the Kandyan kingdom, Mulkirigala in the south and several Buddhist monasteries in the hinterland of Colombo, Galle (Yatagala) and Matara are all places of great antiquity retaining the principal elements of their rock-shelter, boulder-and-terrace garden complexes through the vicissitudes of the post-classic era. They emerge in the 18th and 19th centuries as persistent survivals of ancient garden design, bearing the unmistakable signs of the various periods of their multi-layered histories. These examples provide the opportunity to study in a living form archetypal Sri Lankan garden types that have lasted over centuries.

A parallel garden tradition, one that also looks back to horizons prior to the 18th century, is to be seen in the courtyard gardens of the *valavvas*, the urban or rural manorial houses of the secular, landlord-official elite. Many of these buildings (suburban or rural manors or urban mansions or villas) have survived from the 18th and 19th centuries in the Kandyan territories, in the southwest maritime region around the southern cities of Galle and Matara and in the northern peninsula of Jaffna, each region displaying its own distinct variants. In the Kandyan area, the monastic residences in Buddhist temples also preserve the courtyard form

This 18th-century painting by a Dutch artist shows the royal city of Kandy and its man-made lake as it was before the British conquest in 1815. The Temple of the Tooth-Relic and the royal palace are situated in the foreground on the right.
Artist unknown. The painting is on display in a restaurant in the old city of Kandy.

resembling those in the manorial houses. Although the surviving gardens are from relatively recent times (not earlier than the 18th century), there is good reason to consider them an archetypal form of considerable antiquity, whose precise origins and development only archaeology will be able to retrieve.

The historical tradition reaches its final expression in the grand designed landscape of the royal city of Kandy, which attains its most substantial expansion under the last Kandyan kings, between 1747 and 1815 (see below, chapter 2). The surrender of Kandy marks the colonial occupation of the entire country, lasting for a period of nearly one-and-half centuries.

The colonial encounter and the modern transition

The archaeology and history of Sri Lankan gardens is incomplete without some consideration of the living garden forms of the last two or three hundred years. These gardens contribute to the understanding of tradition and the interpretation of archaeological remains. From about the late 17th century important changes begin to take place in Sri Lankan society, economy, and daily life, culminating in the fundamental transformations of the late 19th and 20th centuries under British colonial rule. The development of plantation agriculture, first coffee, then tea, coconut, and rubber, created entirely new agricultural landscapes and road and rail infrastructure, and ultimately brought about demographic transitions that affected the entire cultural landscape in a variety of ways and in many different contexts. The complex response to colonial hegemony is reflected in the creation of gardens and landscapes, paralleling developments in other fields of cultural activity. It includes the imposition and absorption of colonial garden forms, the resistance, revival and re-interpretation of tradition and, after the regaining of political independence in 1948, modernist innovation, the latter resulting in the formation of a distinctive Sri Lankan 'modernism' in garden design.

Initially, the colonial encounter seems to have resulted in the attempted introduction or replication

The Dutch governor's residence and garden in the Fort of Colombo. Watercolour, C. Steiger, c. 1710, Rjiksmuseum Amsterdam

of baroque garden designs imported from Europe or of mixed origins. One of the earliest representations of a garden from a colonial context is a mid-17th-century pictorial map of Colombo, showing a formal eight-sectioned European garden with symmetrically arranged trees behind the residence of the Dutch governor in the Fort of Colombo. Pictorial evidence, literary descriptions and scant but visible material remains at the site allow us to conjecture a classic Franco-Dutch garden that existed here for more than a hundred years, a garden that was, at least until a few years ago, archaeologically retrievable. Judging by contemporary engravings, the parterres of this garden have the style of an 18th-century European garden, presumably using Sri Lankan planting material, as seen in a sketch from 1805 by the British landscapist-botanist Alexander Moon.

No other pre-modern colonial gardens have survived even in a vestigial form. The colonial encounter under British hegemony, however, gave rise to various new garden forms.

Firstly, to botanic gardens and parks. The varied Sri Lankan ecosystems provided ideal conditions for research and experimentation in tropical botany. Several botanical gardens were established, linked with the development of plantation agriculture for the mass production of tropical crops in a booming global economy. Peradeniya, Hakgala, and Heneratgoda are the impressive survivors of these early ventures, epitomised, we might say, by Alexander Moon's elegant plan of 1815 for the garden he visualised at Peradeniya even before the complete British takeover of the Kandyan kingdom in 1818. From a botanical, as well as from a

An example of a Tea Estate garden from around 1910at Roehampton Estate near Bandarawela. It is a particularly well-designed garden in the British Arts & Crafts style. Historic photo from the 1920s, conserved inside the bungalow.
Photographer unknown.

The so-called Kandy House, situated in the countryside near Kandy. It is a typical 18th-century Singhalese manorial Walawwa surrounded by a garden. This example has recently been restored and transformed into a hotel.

conceptual and artistic point of view, the Royal Botanic Garden of Peradeniya is the most notable with his rich variety of garden scenes, some of them showing strong Victorian influence.

Secondly, the large estates with bungalows, surrounded by gardens, of a landowning and entrepreneurial class, that flourished between 1860 and 1930. They appear to be mainly derived from an imported or hybrid manor house or urban villa style, with single or double gateways, a formal symmetrical or winding driveway leading to a portico and an extensive front lawn, the entire formula interpreted to suit Sri Lankan conditions. The garden area on either side of the grand lawn was a tree-covered space echoing the traditional Sri Lankan house garden, while the garden behind the house was a typical, large and often untidy kitchen and service area. Although a disappearing species, many such mansion gardens still survive.

Among these estates we shall recall two contrasting examples: Roehampton Estate Garden near Haputale and Richmond Castle at Kalutara. The first, created at the dawn of the 20th century, still retains significant elements of the Gertrude Jekyll Arts & Crafts movement style with all its ingredients. The second, dating from the same period, is a typical example of eclecticism, both the mansion and the garden, but a quite peculiar one. Here we see how a wealthy and important Singhalese notable sought to make an impression on the elite of his kind by imitating a Maharaja friend's Moghul Garden which he had visited in India.

The third garden form was the creation of public spaces, 'imported' garden forms in an 'English style', often combined with a monumental neo-classical architecture, especially those attached to official buildings such as the new Town Hall in Colombo, the National Museum, the Legislative Council (now 'President's House'), but also to schools, temples or churches. A typical example, found in the Jaffna Province, is the Uduvil Girls' School. The largest public space in today's Colombo is the Galle Face Green, facing the ocean. Now a public park, it was created between 1856 and 1859 mainly for sports use.

National resurgence

The social and economic transformations of this period and the developing plantation and entrepreneurial economy also propelled the national resurgence and the resistance to colonial hegemony, not only in the political but also in the cultural and religious spheres, with significant impact on the evolution of garden and landscape design. The Buddhist revival and the national movement of the 19th century saw the re-emergence of a deeply embedded art of site selection and site planning in many new urban, suburban and rural monasteries, especially in the southern and western maritime regions that, at least instinctively and subconsciously, drew on the memory of ancient garden traditions. The landscaping of these sites and the accompanying ornamental horticulture are so varied and organic that they defy systematisation without extensive field research. Nevertheless even a casual survey of the myriad combinations of flowering trees and shrubs, foliage and potted plants, sand courtyards, site topography and level changes presents a specific Sri Lankan garden style that merits careful documentation and study by garden historians.

This style is frequently paralleled in the house gardens in rural, urban and suburban contexts, which display an equally organic form right across the social spectrum. The traditional domestic house, whether the cottage of the peasant farmer or the manorial *Walawwa* usually stood in its own garden, an open treeless inner demarcated space immediately around the building, with potted plants and flowering shrubs, and a tree-covered outer garden.

A variation of this is sometimes called the 'forest garden'. This is a concentration, within a relatively limited extent of ground, of a profusion of trees and plants of various kinds, both cultivated and organically generated, or shade bearing, or merely ornamental, populated by both indigenous and exotic species, to form a miniature, man-made forest. Ironically one of the rare, succinct descriptions of such a garden is a mid-19th century account of a derelict garden of a former Dutch colonial governor in the southern city of Galle:

> The neglected garden, with its decaying terraces [...] contains Indian fruit trees and plants almost returned to their primitive wildness. Oranges, custard apples, bread-fruits, bilimbis, and bananas are mingled with the crimson hibiscus and innumerable other flowering

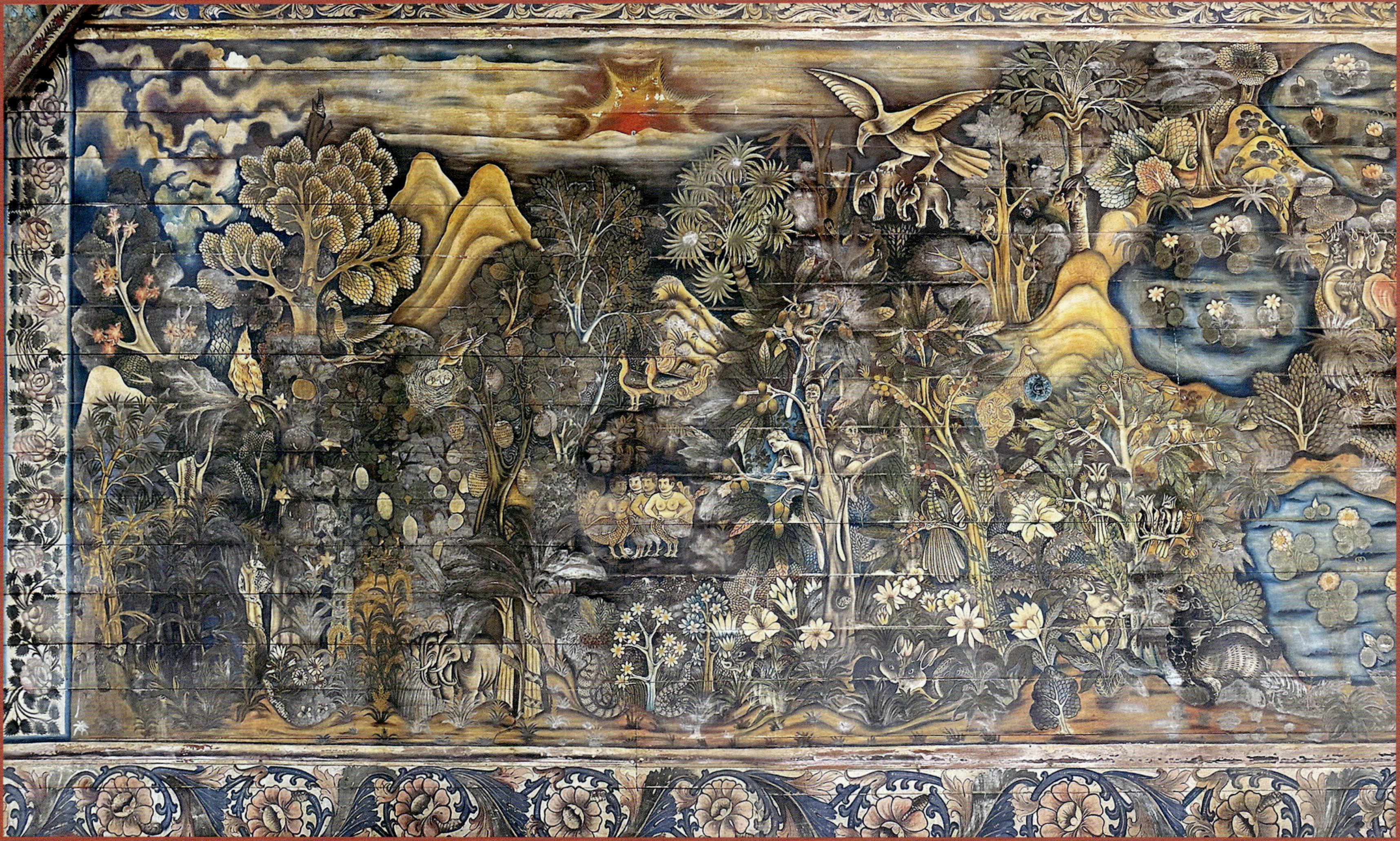

A very large wall painting in the Rankot Vihare at Panadura, early 20th century. A rare example of an idealised cosmological landscape showing nature at its most resplendent with an incredible richness of details. *Photos Daniel Oertli Lausanne, photocomposition Ivan Baranowski Zurich.*

Top:
Another typically Buddhist scene from the same Rankot Vihare at Panadura.
Photos Daniel Oertli Lausanne, photocomposition Ivan Baranowski Zurich.

Bottom:
Wall painting showing a garden with a bathing pool, 19th century, at the Mulkirigala temple in the southern province.

> shrubs, whose branches were covered with exquisite climbing plants, clitoriae and convolvuli; and beneath their moist shade grew innumerable balsams in all their endless varieties of colour.[14]

James Emerson Tennent's description reminds us that Sinhala poetry of all periods is replete with descriptions and celebrations of nature, showing the Sri Lankan sensitivity to the natural world. This is a particularly distinctive feature of the so-called 'messenger' poems written between about the 13th and early 19th centuries, where a message is carried from one place to another by a bird that, during its flight, describes the countryside below.[15] However, the most evocative documentary presentations of the perennial Sri Lankan garden tradition come from contemporary 18th and 19th century paintings rather than from texts. Although trees and groves are often depicted in the murals of this period, it is the rare examples of highly imaginative cosmological Himalayan landscapes, which combine topography, mountains, man-made water features, rivers, streams, trees and flowers, that give expression to the sensibilities and concepts underlying Sri Lankan garden tradition. What we see in these Sri Lankan murals is something very different from the gardens in Indian miniature paintings: they are less elegant but also grander, wilder and more powerful. Foreign visual and literary records of royal and other gardens are few and far between but sometimes provide information at a level of detail not available in other sources. Garden archaeology opens up a whole new field in the study of the Sri Lankan imaginative landscape in historical times, beginning at Anuradhapura.

Contemporary interpretations

The organic developments of the early modern transition in the period of colonial occupation and national resurgence laid the foundations for the revival of a conscious tradition of innovative modern garden design in the latter half of the 20th century, closely associated with the emergence of a Sri Lankan style of modern architecture. An eccentric and dramatic prefiguring of this can be seen in the work of one of the earliest modern garden designers in Sri Lanka, a Frenchman, Maurice Talvande, Count de Mauny Talvande (1866-1941) who, between the 1920s and 1940s, built for himself a diminutive neo-Palladian villa and exquisite garden on a small island in Weligama Bay, off the south-western coast, which he called *Taprobane*. A talented gardener and garden designer, Talvande achieved a certain influence through the two books he published, *Gardening in Ceylon*, in 1921, a collection of general horticultural observations and critical comments, with interesting photographs of Sri Lankan gardens from 1910-1920, and *The Gardens of Taprobane*, in 1937, a diary of his own experience in making his garden on the island. The villa and the garden still survive, albeit with many changes. From his own description, and from what remains, we can conclude that *Taprobane* is essentially an interpretation of an ornamental Sri Lankan 'forest garden', with some Italianate elements, a lawn terrace, and a profusion of foliage plants and flowering trees and shrubs, entirely surrounding and enclosing the house. Talvande is also credited with horticultural consulting for other gardens and acquired a reputation for his critical analysis of parts of the Peradeniya botanical gardens.

The second half of the 20th century witnessed a major revival of interest in imaginative garden design, especially inspired by the brothers Bevis and Geoffrey Bawa, who have left behind their own personal gardens, *Brief* and *Lunuganga*. Bevis Bawa, a talented autodidact, over the years transformed a former rubber plantation into a succession of surprising garden spaces with strong individual atmospheres, the *Brief*.

Geoffrey Bawa is best known for his architecture in which the buildings are closely interwoven with gardens and water features. He reinterpreted the garden schemes of the traditional domestic house, opening the house out into the garden and bringing the garden into the house. He took great care in selecting plant material, especially the bold use of foliage plants. His thirty-year 'encounter' with *Lunuganga*, the elaborate lakeside garden complex he fashioned around his country house at Bentota, epitomises these interests. At the same time, it also displays his early eclecticism and the inspiration he derived from such disparate traditions as the Italian Renaissance, the English landscape garden and the rural Sri Lankan garden scenery, as well as the ancient royal and monastic garden art. In Bawa's later and more formal projects, as much as in many parts of *Lunuganga* itself, he combined trees, water, garden areas and architectural spaces in an approach oftent reminescent of the garden landscapes of Anuradhapura, Sigiriya and Polonnaruwa, but in an entirely fresh and modern way. His courtyard water gardens are amongst his most original creations, yet they fit easily and perfectly into a continuing Sri Lankan tradition. This is even more emphatically the case with the second-generation gardens of this 'Bawa school', such as Laki Senanyake's Diyabubula near Dambulla and Lalyn Collure's Boulder Garden Hotel near Kalawana, and many others, where the wheel turns full circle and the boulder and forest gardens find purely modern – yet perennial – expression. The complete liberation of form, within a given framework of topography, flora and history, marks modern Sri Lankan gardens, as much as it distinguishes itself from the boulder-and-terrace gardens of early historic times.

A contemporary water garden at the main entrance to the Triton Hotel at Ahungalla on the south-west coast, designed by Geoffrey Bawa, 1981. The current name of the hotel is Heritance Ahungalla Hotel.

SURPRISE IN GARDENS

Gianni Biaggi

Finally, as a complementing way to appreciate gardens in Sri Lanka, an approach through the concept of 'surprise' can be refreshing. Surprise is a vast and universal phenomenon that captures our senses, primarily the visual secondarily the others. It can be experienced by everyone, in a direct and non mediated way regardless of cultural preparation, who undergoes a kinesthetic experience by strolling in a garden or other environments. Visual surprise arises when the components of an environment – the centre of gravity, the horizon line, the visual gradients of objects, the sudden change of topography – are suddenly jostled. Surprise can thus be defined as the result of instantaneous modifications of our perceptions knowingly felt by an individual who moves around in a garden, a building, a city, ecc, reproducible with lesser intensity, and which provoke a phase of excitement, followed by a sense of awe and marvel. This occurs in particular by the alternation between the hidden and the revealed – the Japanese concept of Miegakure.

Gardens in Sri Lanka are the ideal locus of surprise, due to the accidental topography of the country and the great quantity of boulders as a major feature. They are unique and, as the Japanese and Chinese models, transcend the stylistic classical and romantic approach to gardens of Western civilisation.

1 The term garden, a part of the title of this book, is used here to signify an extent of land in which humans have selectively or totally ordered the deployment or development of trees, plants, shrubs, grasses or mosses, and sometimes other natural features such as water, sand, rocks, boulders, caves, etc., in such a way that a conceptual and intentional human 'redesign' of the natural world is detectable in the overall arrangement of that extent of land. A garden can be an integrated or added element to an architectural layout, in which it is 'subservient' to the architecture; or it can be an independent entity without any architectural dimension, or the principal, or equally distinctive, element in a combination of architecture and garden. It is important to emphasise that the term garden cannot be applied to every space, wholly or partially open to the sky, and demarcated by architectural features, or by an arrangement of natural elements created or defined, knowingly or unknowingly, by human activity. However, it is sometimes difficult to make the distinction between what is a garden and what is not. 'Designed landscape' is an old term whose use has been revived. It is used to designate a usually large extent of territory which has been modified from its natural state, consciously or unconsciously, by human activity. All gardens, we might say, are designed landscapes but not all designed landscapes are gardens. Gardens usually have defined boundaries – defined by buildings, walls, rows of trees or water features such as lakes, pools or moats.

2 The Yuan Ming Yuan is 10 kilometres in circumference and covers an area of 365 hectares. This is nearly half the size of Versailles, which is 800 hectares with its outlying parklands and forests.

3 The terminology used in this connection throughout the book is based on a hierarchy of meaning and reference, reflecting an increasing degree of human intervention in an originally natural situation, thus the sequence: forest – grove – park – garden. Although the distinctions between these forms may not be easy to define, the varying deployment of trees and plants in each category is not difficult to visualise on the ground.

4 The critical view that these echo canonical accounts of early Buddhist history in the Gangetic region does not mean that the strong, oral and textual historiographical traditions of Sri Lankan Buddhists are not authentic 'reflections' of how these events really took place.

5 Although rocks and boulders have been associated with gardens and architecture in many cultures, especially in religious and royal contexts, the identification of the Boulder Garden as a distinct garden form and the invention and application of the term itself seem to have been a product of archaeological research at Sigiriya in the 1980s and '90s.

6 Anthropologists and historians have long observed that the role of the king as rainmaker is common to many cultures in various forms. For a succinct survey of its historical importance in Sri Lanka see Disanayaka 1992, 51-56.

7 *Mv* 10.83. For the entire description of the founding and layout of the city of Anuradhapura by the semi-historical figure of Pandukhabhaya, the grandfather of King Devanampiya Tissa (250-210 BCE), see *Mv* 10.73-102.

8 'In the final analysis, we may say that while Sinhala poetry adopted the conventions of garden and water sports, which were an essential element in a Sanskrit [epic] poem, they successfully invested it with an originality drawn from personal experience and adapted it creatively to suit the actual traditions and environment of the country. The concrete manifestation of their experience is present, on the one hand, in the archaeological remains of ancient pleasure and water gardens and, on the other, in contemporary bathing practises.

9 Trans. after Harold Peiris and Len van Geyzel.

10 The *Upavanavinoda* is part of the *Sarangadhara Paddhdati*, an anthology of classical Sanskrit texts. While there are no treatises so far discovered on ancient horticulture as such, there is a small chapter, the Upavanavinoda as a branch of Vrksayurveda, in Sarangadhara's encyclopaedic work, the *Sarangadhara Paddhati* of the 13th Century, which is a compilation of relevant material from earlier classical sources.

11 Paranavitana 1944, 193.

12 Paranavitana 1954, 29.

13 EZ 1, 35-36.

14 Tennent 1859, vol. 2, 105.

15 See Godakumbura 1955.

Chronology of Sri Lanka's history

<table>
<tr><td>20000 BCE – 10000 BCE</td><td colspan="2">Prehistoric period</td><td colspan="2">Mesolithic</td><td rowspan="2">Band and tribal society</td></tr>
<tr><td>10000 BCE – 1000 BCE</td><td colspan="2">Protohistoric period</td><td colspan="2">Sedentary, iron age, farming, irrigation</td></tr>
<tr><td>300 BCE
250 BCE – 210 BCE</td><td colspan="2" rowspan="2">Early Anuradhapura period
King Devanampiyatissa
Arahat Mahinda brings Buddhism from India to Sri Lanka</td><td rowspan="3">Early historic period</td><td rowspan="6">Primary urbanisation
Major irrigation, architectural complexes, urbanisation</td><td rowspan="6">Unification of the entire island under a kingdom with regional divisions
Centripetal tendencies dominant
End of united kingdom</td></tr>
<tr><td>470</td></tr>
<tr><td>477 – 495</td><td colspan="2">King Kasyapa
Sigiriya period</td></tr>
<tr><td>600 – 1150</td><td colspan="2">Late Anuradhapura period</td><td rowspan="3">Middle historic period</td></tr>
<tr><td>1150 – 1300</td><td colspan="2">Polonnaruwa period</td></tr>
<tr><td>1154 – 1186</td><td colspan="2">King Parakramabahu I</td></tr>
<tr><td>1300 – 1500</td><td colspan="2">Shifting capitals</td><td rowspan="3">Late historic period</td><td rowspan="2">Secondary urbanisation</td><td rowspan="3">Multiple policies,
centrifugal tendencies,
anticolonial wars,
partial occupation</td></tr>
<tr><td>1500 – 1653
1505
1639</td><td>Kotte period</td><td>Arrival of the Portuguese
Portuguese occupation
Arrival of the Dutch</td></tr>
<tr><td>1653 – 1815
1796
1815</td><td>Kandy period</td><td>Dutch occupation
British conquest of Ceylon
End of Kandy kingdom</td><td>Tertiary urbanisation
Beginning of modern transition</td></tr>
<tr><td>1815 – 1948</td><td colspan="3">Total colonial occupation by the British Empire</td><td colspan="2">British administration,
destruction of the tropical rainforest for tea and rubber plantations,
introduction of many exotic trees,
construction of modern infrastructure (roads, railways)</td></tr>
<tr><td>1948 – today</td><td colspan="3">Independence of modern Sri Lanka</td><td colspan="2">Post-colonial architecture</td></tr>
</table>

Reference: *Continuities and Transformations*, Senake Bandaranayake; Social Scientists' Association 2012 (p. 126, fig. 4.2).
This chronology is reflecting an archeologist's point of view and has been adapted for this book. May be a historian could see it a little different.

Places of interest mentioned in this book

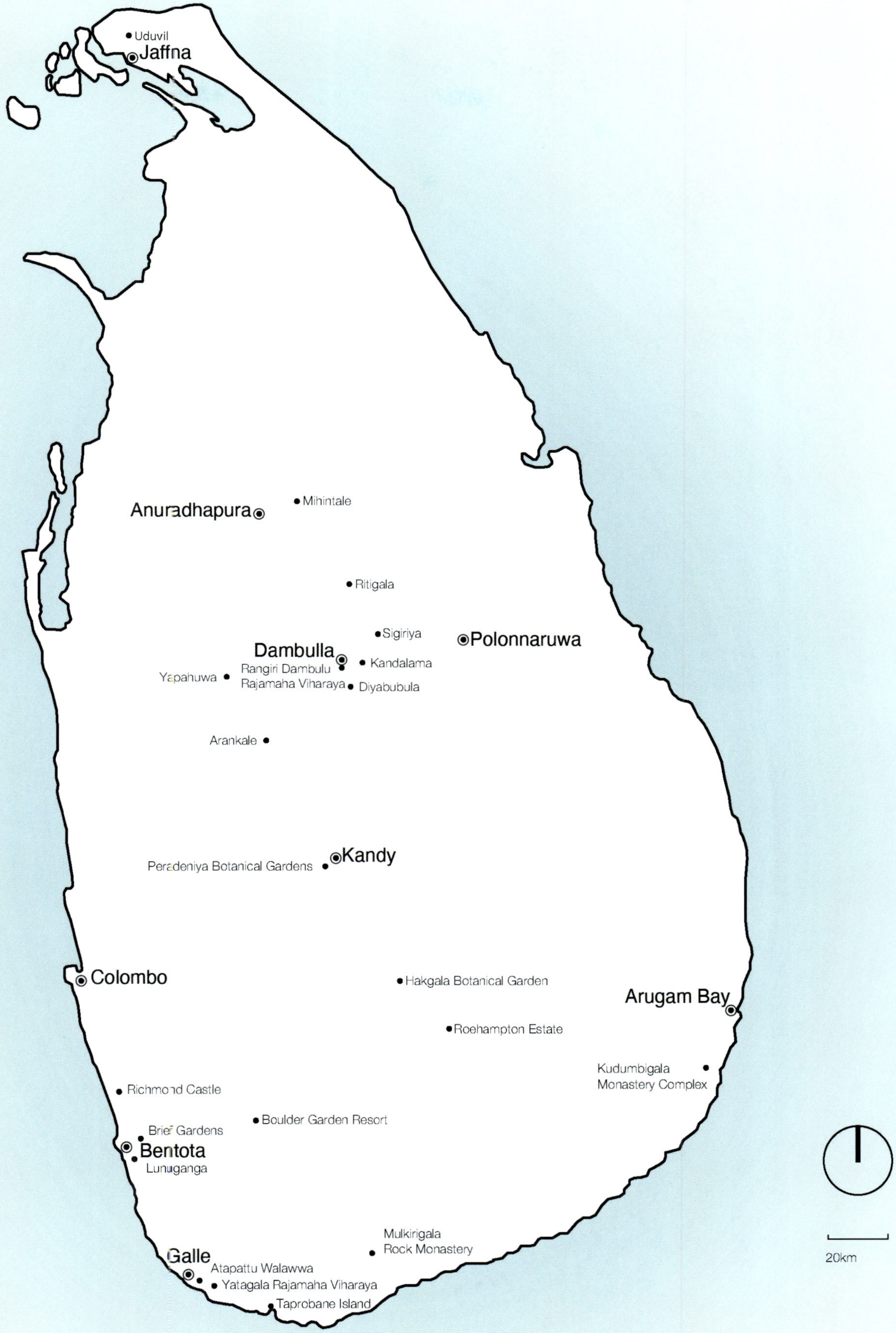

The last royal gardens of the Singhalese kings at Kandy, the last royal city, 1653–1815. A man-made lake surrounded by a lace-like ornamental parapet wall with an island on which stood a pavilion within a garden.

Royal Gardens

Prof. Senake Bandaranayake

Introduction

It is remarkable that despite the importance attached to gardens in the Mahavamsa *Chronicle* (in lists of major works attributed to successive rulers), neither historians nor archaeologists have paid much attention to garden remains in their surveys of Sri Lanka's past. While surviving gardens seem limited when compared with architecture or sculpture, the history of royal garden design clearly parallels the evolution of other Sri Lankan art forms, from the overarching symmetries of Sigiriya to the complex irregularity of Kandy, from the formalised realism of Early and Middle Historic times to the stylisation and informality of the Late Historic era (see Chronology, p. 32).

The Sri Lankan royal capitals of all periods were almost always located on the shores of man-made lakes. Anuradhapura, with its ring of encircling lakes, marks the ancient epicentre of this tradition. The lakeside location is best seen today at Polonnaruwa where the rampart walls of the inner and outer cities are on the edge of the 'Sea of Parakrama', the 12th century amalgamation of three smaller artificial lakes carried out during the reign of Parakramabahu I (1153-1186). Several centuries later, this appears on a much smaller scale, but in a still living form, in Kandy in the 18th and 19th centuries.

However, despite evidence from inscriptions and other historical and literary sources and a sizeable archaeological record of garden layouts in monastic contexts, so far we have significant vestiges of only four royal gardens, spanning a period of more than two millennia:

- the long-surviving Ranmasu Uyana, 'the Goldfish Park', in Anuradhapura, in its present form from about the 10th century CE, but originally part of an early monastic settlement of the last few centuries BCE;

- the even earlier, unique, 5th-century gardens at Sigiriya;
- the fragments and traces of the 12th- and 13th-century Dipuyana, the 'Garden of Islands' in Polonnaruwa;
- the designed landscape of the lake city of Kandy in the 18th and 19th centuries.

These remains provide us with a very limited body of evidence regarding the nature of royal gardens over a millennial timeframethat extends from the ancient royal parks at Anuradhapura in the last few centuries BCE, at one end, to the interrupted development of Kandy's 19th-century designed landscape at the other. The large gaps in this trajectory may seem unbridgeable in our present state of knowledge, but this is primarily the result of a lack of archaeological interest and focus. This neglect is also influenced by other factors which directly affected the material remains – such as changes in the nature of patronage, technology and the use of materials, the sustainability of the surviving gardens, and the vicissitudes of the socio-economic and political conditions underlying the long and complex post-Polonnaruwa epoch (see 'Shifting Capitals' chapter, p. 88).

Anuradhapura

Anuradhapura was an urban settlement and subsequently a royal centre from about the 5th or 4th century BCE, if not earlier, and Sri Lanka's principal city for nearly 1,500 years. In the *Chronicle* records relating to the formation of the city we see a considerable degree of importance attached to the royal parks on its periphery. These parks, along with tree-shrines associated with traditional deities such as the Banyan Tree of the God of Wealth and the Palmyra Tree of the Demon of Maladies, were donated to the Buddhist monastic order. They were developed over a period of two millennia as the principal centres of Sri Lankan Buddhist tradition.

In its most developed form Anuradhapura was a walled and moated city set in a cultural landscape of forested parks and groves, suburban and rural settlements, man-made lakes, road networks and centres of ritual, eremitical and monastic activity. At first glance, this many-layered antiquity itself obscures the presence of garden remains as a significant element in its urban form. The major urban monasteries – starting with the Mahavihara in the Mahamegha Royal Park just outside the southern gate of the city – were established in and around the forests, parklands and settlements encircling the fortified urban core.

The city and the ancient monasteries developed over the centuries, reaching their maximum spread between the 9th and 13th centuries. From about the 13th and 14th centuries onwards there was a demographic shift from the Dry Zone plains of the northern half of the country to the southwest, the central mountains and the extreme north, leading ultimately to the abandonment, decay and destruction of the greater part of the city's monuments.

The retrieval of this heritage was the major focus of archaeological and restorationist activity from the late 18th and 19th centuries and it is a continuing process to this day. For the most part it revealed the surface and sub-surface fragments that we see today in many places in and around the abandoned ancient urban complex freed of debris, topsoil and invasive forest cover. The monastic elements – especially the ruins around Anuradhapura's colossal stupas – dominated the new cultural landscape, which reverted to what could have been something like its ancient parkland character. We read them today as shadows of their historic past, most of it deeply buried under stratified deposits evidenced everywhere in excavations in and around the city. It is at a location in the southernmost spread of the 'suburban' settlements around the city that we find the only surviving remains of a royal park in Anuradhapura, the Ranmasu Uyana. This complex is a component part of the ancient monastic settlement, the Issarasamanaramavihara.

The Issarasamanarama sequence

This sequence is perhaps the only survivor of Anuradhapura's ancient royal parks whose archaeological remains are still visible on the surface. It lies in the southern sector of Anuradhapura and takes its place as a component of a larger designed landscape, about 3,500m in length, extending from the remains of the present Vessagiriya monastery in the south to the Ranmasu Uyana in the north. It is a terrace-and-boulder garden complex, whose ancient name Issarasamanarama is preserved in the name of the modern temple applied in a modified popular form to its central component, the still venerated 'Isurumuniya' Vihara.

The identification and conservation of the Ranmasu Uyana, the Royal Goldfish Park, in Anuradhapura in the 1940s, mark the beginnings of garden archaeology and garden history in Sri Lanka.

For the first time part of an interconnected group of ruined structures was identified as the remains of a garden, and the name of the garden confirmed by inscriptional evidence. Although not conceived on the grand scale of Sigiriya, the Ranmasu Uyana is a rarity in the Sri Lankan context, as a pure, walled garden

Top:
The landscape of the ancient city of Anuradhapura is still today surrounded by man-made lakes and dominated by the colossal old stupas, some as high as 120 m.

Bottom:
The Issarasamanarama sequence seen from the south. In the foreground are the boulders of the old Vessagiriya monastery, to the left the Tissawava lake.

The same Issarasamanarana sequence seen from the north. In the foreground the Ranmasu Uyana royal garden, in the middle the Isurumuniya Vihara and in the background the Vessagiriya monastery. The Tissawava lake is to the right.

The Isurumuniya Vihara seen from the west and from the east.

space, not 'subordinated' (at least in its overall plan) to a palace or monastery complex.

The complex is centred on the present Isurumuniya monastery. This entire sequence is oriented on a north-south axis determined by the geological formation of underlying proterozoic bedrock of gneissic-granite, which extends like a finger along that axis. The bedrock surfaces at three locations in the form of great boulder clusters of the most extraordinary landscape formations, emerging from the plain of what were the southern suburbs of the ancient city.

To the west of this boulder sequence, immediately abutting the Isurumuni Vihara and the Ranmasu Uyana, and running parallel to the rocky outcrop, rises the towering earth dam of the Tisavava lake, one of the four ancient man-made lakes sustaining the metropolis. It would appear that the three boulder clusters, and the area between them, formed the ancient Issarasamana Vihara, one of the earliest Buddhist monastic settlements in Anuradhapura of about the 3rd to 1st centuries BCE. The Vessagiriya and Isurumuniya sites show a continuity of occupation over centuries, extending from prehistoric times.

Ranmasu Uyana

The Issarasamanarama, even in its relict and fractured form today, presents one of the most distinctive boulder-and-water garden sequences in Sri Lanka, marked by design concepts of great beauty and intricacy. Although a detailed reconstruction of the history of the site must await further archaeological investigation, it is likely that by the 10th century the three sites formed three distinct architectural and landscape formations. As it is today, the Ranmasu Uyana is roughly rectangular in shape, more than 1,150m in length from north to south and about 600m at its widest from east to west. Originally a walled garden, it is bounded on the north, south and east by the vestigial remains of a brick wall with stone foundations, and on the west by the earth dam of the Tisavava lake.

The garden was laid out in an inspired combination of axial, sectional and three-dimensional planning, its north-south axial orientation emphasised in four parallel formations: the high earth dam of the Tisavava, with its (presumably) tree-covered slopes on the west, its foot is lasting against the boulder range; the colossal, 'sculptural' boulder formations in the centre, with the stone baths; the three linear rectangular 'goldfish and lotus' ponds (*diguvil*) on the east; and, defining the eastern limits of the garden, the vestigial boundary wall with an entrance gatehouse and an archaeologically un-excavated flat area of ground, occupied today by rice paddies. A modern irrigation canal, accompanied by coconut palms, parallel to the ponds, indicates that there may once have been along this eastern boundary a moated water feature and other water garden elements or a tree-lined park with a stream running through it.

At the northern extremity of the garden are two almost square ponds, one of them with an island terrace, entered from the south, hemmed in by low rock formations to the east and southeast. The island forms an elevated platform on which stand the ruined bases of three octagonal pavilions, the largest in the middle and two, smaller matching structures on either side. A gatehouse provides access to the terrace. The easternmost extent of the garden is marked by the vestigial remains of a structure which may also have been a gatehouse, aligned roughly with the centre of the boulder formation.

An aerial view of the Ranmasu Uyana reveals the intricate planning of the water gardens. The garden appears as a three-dimensional form, a 'floating' rectangular space

The Ranmasu Uyana royal garden at the foot of the 2000-year-old Tissawava lake dam seen from the east.

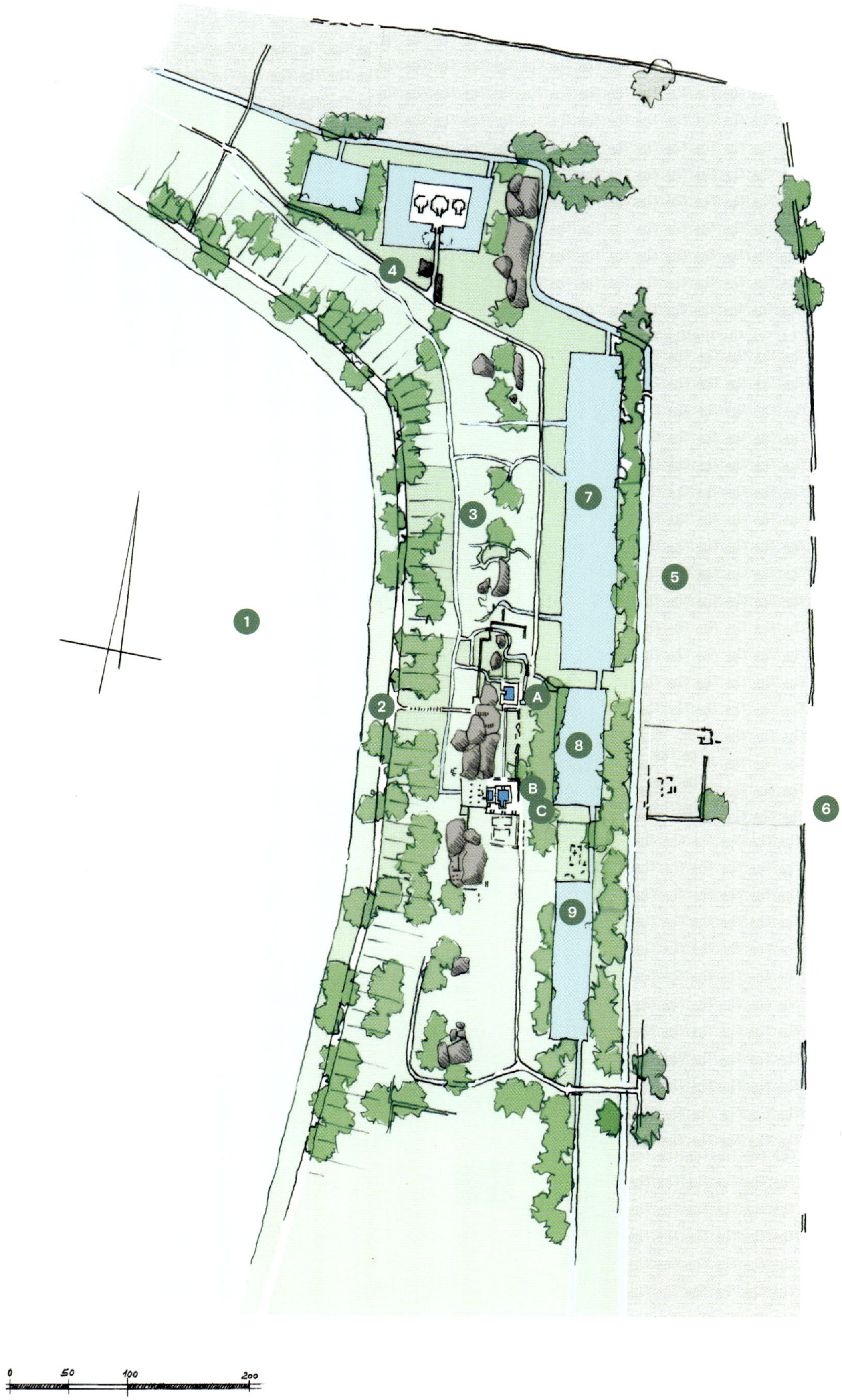

RANMASU UYANA

A Bath A with Elephant relief
B Bath B
C Bath C
1 Tissawava Lake
2 Lake dam
3 Water supply channel
4 Northern ponds and ruins
5 Unexcavated ancient park area
6 Ancient boundary wall
7 Northern pond/vila
8 Central pond/vila
9 Southern pond/vila

Drawing: Klaus Holzhausen, based on measurements on the site by the author
Source: *Landscape Tradition of Sri Lanka,* Nimal De Silva 1996, p. 34

in an area marked by a high dam. Water bodies emerge, formed at the level of the boulder clusters. Varied architectural forms and surrounding tree-covered parklands in the garden space would be visible from the bund of the tank, and the pavilions and towers perched on top of the boulders offered a visual relation with the waters of the Tissawava at the west and the eastern and northern landscape, dominated by the great stupas around the city and the Mihintale mountains to the east, while the main part of the park is situated much below the lake. The stone baths at the foot of the boulders are situated at a higher level (ca. 2 m) than the bottom of the park. From there the view over the lotus ponds and until the eastern boundary is more intimate.

The most dramatic feature of the garden when viewed from a distance is the central boulder formation, massive rocks set in a gently undulating terrain, a startling natural feature turned into a designed garden landscape dominated by a rock garden on a colossal scale. The two clusters of the central formation are designated 'Rocks Y' and 'Rocks Z' in the early archaeological reports. On entering the garden and approaching the boulders for a closer view, we see that immediately attached to them on the east is a sequence of stone bathing pools designated 'Bath A', 'Bath 'B', and 'Bath C'. In their own way the pools are as dramatic as the boulders.

The principal design feature of these pools is their 'chaste geometry' offset by the natural topography of the boulders and the surrounding terrain – a remarkable combination of symmetry and asymmetry. The pools have stone-paved floors and descending tiers made of dressed granite slabs with classic linear mouldings. The northernmost pool is the largest and deepest and merges with the boulder formation. Lying to the south of the boulder cluster Y are Baths B and C, placed next to each other, the one larger than the other and both shallower than Bath A.

At the northern end of the garden is a rectangular pond with an island, connected by an access dam and a gatehouse. On the island the bases of three octagonal pavilions are visible.

The central part of the garden with the stone baths A and B and C leaning back against the boulder range. The dam of the Tissawava lake is about 10m high.

Detail of stone bath A; above, a water supply channel is visible. To the left are examples of how the tops of some boulders were used for pavilion constructions, with access on the top.

More detailed views of bath A. The chamber in the middle is flanked on both sides by very beautiful bas reliefs of elephants cut into the face of the rock.

The keynote of the whole composition is its simplicity, its ornamentation reduced to a minimum and nowhere applied inappropriately. The proportions of the various parts of each structure and of the different structures in relation to one another are harmonious. The lines are perfect and the stone-work exhibits a finish and technical proficiency of a high order.

Both sets of baths have chambers on the west, facing away from the boulders. The chamber in Bath A is a small recess carved out of bedrock and flanked on either side by bas-relief sculpture, cut in the face of the rock, of elephants sporting in the water amongst lotuses and fish. It is likely that the whole arrangement was activated by water pouring down from the top of the boulder forming an artificial waterfall animating the elephants and creating a water-screen in front of the chamber.

The elephant reliefs are themselves masterpieces of the stone carver's art and epitomise the spirit of a water garden. They are obviously from the same hand or atelier that produced the similarly placed low and high relief sculptures in the 'waterfall' above the central pool at Isurumuniya temple.

The description of the reliefs by British colonial official and first Archaeological Commissioner H.C.P. Bell (1851-1937) is one of the first recorded reactions to this sculptural masterpiece of animal representation:

> [...] wondrously realistic bas-reliefs [...] These represent elephants in a lotus-covered tank. On the rock slope to the right three elephants are shown lazily disporting themselves in the water, undisturbed, amid lotuses and fish. On the left the scene is vividly changed. Some sudden alarm has roused the elephants; one seems to be scenting danger, the other two are already in full flight. [...] This absolutely unique piece of carving is without exception the most spirited and life-like to be seen anywhere among the ruins of Anuradhapura.

The chambers in Baths B and C combine in a larger and more elaborate architectural composition, with a pillared and cornice-decorated façade and entrance stairs with miniature decorated balustrades and guard stones. Reclining stone couches are found at the western corners of the bath and in the chamber and are rare evidence of furniture design of the period.

Next page:
Detailed views of baths B and C. The perfection of the stonework is particularly noteworthy. The metal structures of the chamber of bath C are not originals.

The northern part of the garden. A long rectangular, but not stone-lined pond is the northern one in a succession of three linear ponds, which spread over the entire length of the garden. The linear planted coconut palm trees are not authentic at all! *Photocomposition: Ivan Baranowski, Zurich.*

Far right:
The northern, central and southern linear ponds are full of water plants.

There are indications that the smaller Bath C was crowned by a roofed pavilion, while the stone ceiling of the chamber simulates the architectural construction of a wooden ceiling. Still in place are parts of the hydraulic system by which water from the Tisavava and the main Ranmasu Uyana network was channelled into Bath C. Water flowed through three spouts in the cornice moulding above the façade of the chamber, creating an overhead spill of water in front of the chamber, not unlike the water-screen in Bath A. The chamber was thus an ample reclining space behind the falling water.

As the plans show, a number of small halls and pavilions existed associated with the baths. Only fragments of these structures survive today; they were mostly tiled roofed buildings in brick and timber. Attached to the stone baths or dramatically perched on

Section of a mysterious circular cosmic diagram carved on the face of one of the large boulders, 13th to 16th centuries.

top of boulders they add another dimension to the architectural complexity of the garden design, as do the surviving sections of the network of water channels and conduits. If Isurumuniya lacks the grandeur of Sigiriya, it makes up for it in its technological intricacy.

Almost in the middle of the ancient park space there is a second water feature with a totally different character: three linear, rectangular ponds, a *diguvil*, graded from north to south along the entire length of the park. In contrast to the clean stone baths, here the plants dominate. Natural riparian vegetation, leaves and water lili blossom and lotus cover large parts of the calm water surfaces, alive with birds, amphibians and fish, and in which the trees are reflected. Fresh water, fed by the Tissawava, flows through the ponds from north to south.

The ancient park was certainly also composed of trees, but today's trees are nearly all aleatory. Only a range of seven mango trees along the second pond has been planted following a certain logic. The screen of coconut palms along the canal is very present but not in the least authentic. Nevertheless, today's park is a ruined, but living, extensively maintained garden with a beautiful atmosphere.

One sees at Ranmasu Uyana (and at Vessagiriya as well) the combination of boulder clusters with large open spaces, which were probably once parklands and gardens. At Isurumuniya we have a grand sweep of pools and moats fronting the massive boulder which forms the central core of the Isurumuniya temple. At the Ranmasu Uyana the boulder cluster contains an intricate mix of stone baths and large unlined pools, and the play of waterfalls, water jets and water-screened rock-cut chambers. Considered in its totality, the Ranmasu Uyana–Isurumuniya–Vessagiriya sequence, even in its fractured form, is an outstanding example of the ancient garden designer's art.

It is conventional in contemporary practice to date the Ranmasu Uyana to the 9th-10th centuries. This is based largely on the inscription of Mahinda IV (956-72), from which we know that the Ranmasu Uyana was in use and well established as a royal garden in the latter half of the 10th century. We can also assign to this period the extensive use of well-finished dressed granite (i.e., both 'plain ashlar' and 'moulded ashlar'), which is similar to other construction work of that period.

The bas-reliefs of the elephants in Bath A are usually dated to the 7th-8th centuries on the basis of analogies to the elephant sculptures at Isurumuniya and similar work under the Pallava dynasty in India. The partial use of limestone slabs in the construction of the baths, the replacement of limestone with granite and the addition of brick masonry at a later period indicate more than one phase of construction. Nevertheless, the baths and the attached halls and pavilions we see at the site today belong substantially to a well-integrated single period of development, which we may confidently assign to the 9th-10th centuries.

It is important to address here the connection with Sigiriya. The relationship between Sigiriya and the Vessagiriya-Isurumuniya-Ranmasu Uyana complex goes back to the 5th century. The founder of Sigiriya, Kasyapa I (CE 477-95), established (or re-established) a new monastery, the Bo-Upulvan Vihara, at the ancient Issarasamanarama (Isurumuniya) in the name of his two daughters, the Princesses Bodhi and Upulvan. The name of the monastery has endured for more than 600 years.

Unlike Sigiriya, the landscape design of the Vessagiriya-Isurumuniya-Ranmasu Uyana complex is the product of centuries of evolution and change. Its linear and organic plan is very different in its overall conception from Sigiriya's grand symmetry, but it nevertheless reproduces several details found in the Sigiriya water-and-boulder garden style so that we might reasonably hypothesise that the master landscape designers of Sigiriya were responsible for, or were greatly influenced by, the original 5th-century design of the Bo-Upulvan complex.

A number of design elements are common to both sites: the grand sweep of the outer arm of the double moat at Isurumuniya; the boulder-attached pools reminiscent of the octagonal pool at Sigiriya; and the rock-top boulder pavilions so extensively used at Sigiriya and emulated at all three Issarasamanarama locations. The two sites share other common details such as the use of very similar marble moonstones at Sigiriya and Vessagiriya.

At the same time the final 9th-10th-century design of the Ranmasu Uyana with its axial orientation and elaborate, dressed stone baths presents a very different formulation from the grand manner of the royal gardens at Sigiriya.

If we retain the conventional date of the 9th-10th centuries for the royal garden, we also have to keep in mind that the earlier and later use of the garden was likely. If the cosmic diagram proves to be dated between the 13th and 16th centuries and the beginnings of the garden prior to the 9th century, this gives us a period of between six and ten centuries in which the garden was put to various uses, with a high period of development in the 9th-10th century timeframe.

Anuradhapura is known as one of the longest surviving urban complexes in Asia, and some of its major sites have a continuous history of use of more than twenty-three centuries. We also know from excavations in the gardens at Sigiriya, that the 5th-century gardens there were maintained and modified over a period of nearly 800 years. This makes a long chronology for the Ranmasu Uyana not improbable, but that issue must await stratified excavations and other investigations that will give us a finer reading of the chronology of the site.

Sigiriya

Sigiriya, the 'Lion Mountain', is the classic textbook example of Sri Lankan garden design. It is planned around an unusual Pre-Cambrian geological phenomenon, a colossal rock formation with sheer, perpendicular sides, standing 200 metres above the surrounding plain. It was here that Kasyapa I (477-95 CE) and his master builders built his new capital city, with its gardens, ramparts, moats, palaces and a lake. The highly systematic plan of the three km long Sigiriya complex displays both a startling simplicity and a complex mathematics in its compartmentalisation of space. It is based on a modular grid, formed by a series of rectangles one inside the other, extending east and west of the great central rock. The rock itself forms a central core or centre point surrounded by the irregular but concentric terraced slopes of the hill on which it stands. The distinctive characteristic of the plan is its combination of axial and concentric concepts, of symmetry and asymmetry, of echoes and deviations, and a mastery in combining natural topography, systematic planning and a bold creative vision.whe gardens are a combination of the three basic garden types: extensive, geometrically and symmetrically planned water gardens; asymmetrical organic boulder gardens; and, overlapping these, terrace gardens surrounding the rock. The palace gardens on the summit of the rock combine on a much smaller scale the elements of the three garden forms on the hill slopes and the plain below. On either side of the central water gardens placed in an echo layout are four 'moated islands' with palaces or other constructions and miniature gardens: a complex of moats and ramparts surrounding the site on the east, west and north; a lake and an approximately 12 km long feeder canal supplying the lake.

SIGIRIYA

1 Western main entrance
2 Southern entrance
3 Northern entrance
4 Outer moat
5 Inner moat
6 Outer rampart
7 Middle rampart
8 Inner rampart
9 Water Gardens
10 Summer Palace
11 Boulder Gardens
12 Terrace Gardens
13 Lions Paw terrace
14 Royal Palace complex
15 Sigiriya Lake
16 Inner city
17 Outer city

Sources :
• Reproduction of the plan from the Sigiriya Museum Catalogue 2011, adapted and completed by the author
• Sigiriya, city, palace, gardens, monasteries, paintings. Senake Bandaranayake 2005, publication of the Central Cultural Fund

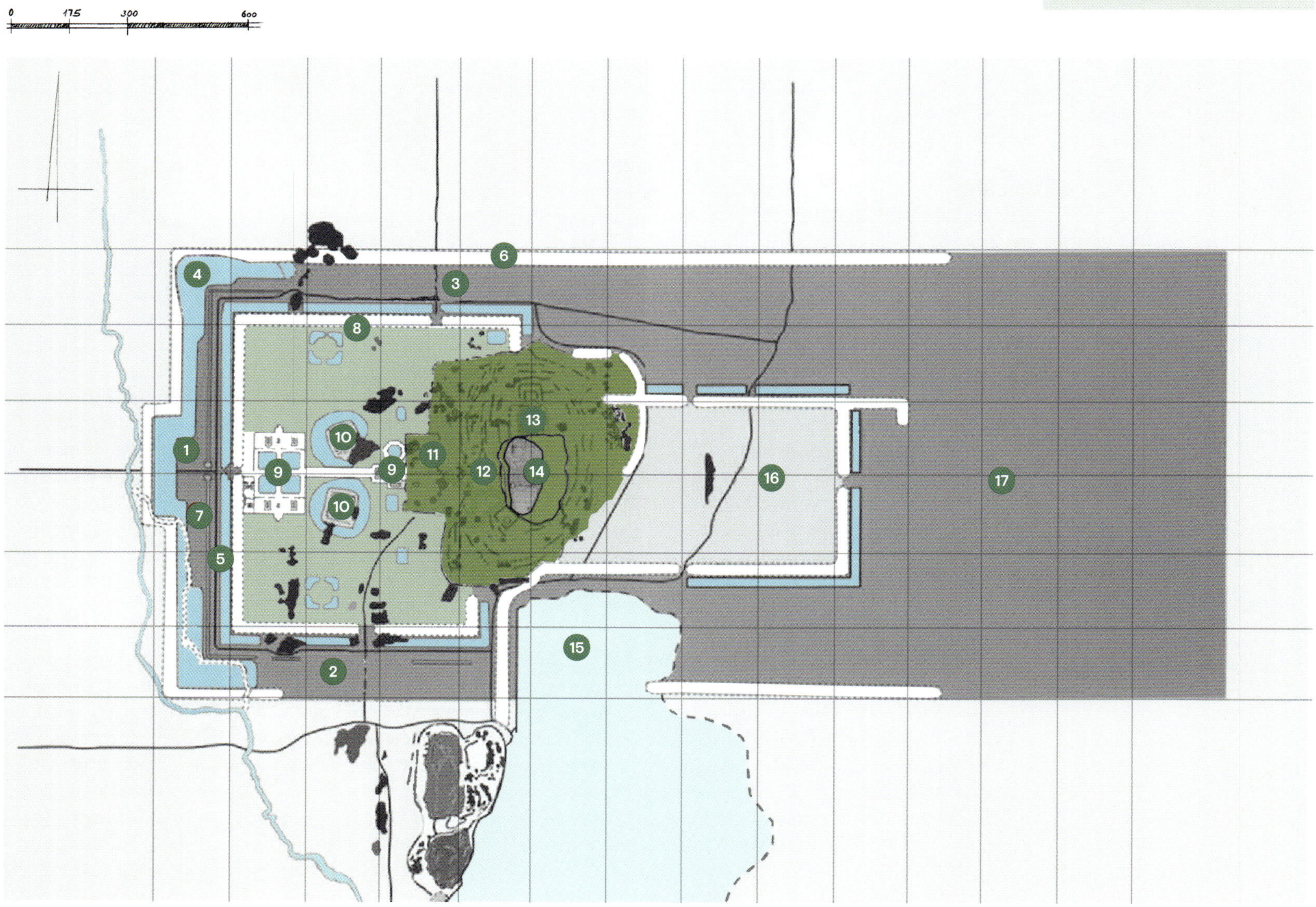

Morning view of the water garden from the west, exactly on the main east-west axis. In the foreground, the inner moat and the western entrance.

A general view of the 900 x 800 m moated water garden west of the rock. The inner moat is clearly visible; of the outer moat only fragments remain. The modern building to the left is the Sigiriya Museum.

The south-western angle of the inner moat.

At Sigiriya, illusion and surprise begin with a sequence along the west-east axis of the garden, when the visitor enters the gate. There is first a progressive interplay between concealment and revelation of the massive rock and the palace, due to the visual obstruction of the inner rampart, and no suggestion yet of a formal garden inside.
After passing the perfectly symmetrical square compound – a *char bagh* type – and the pleasure garden, the stroller progressively approaches a slopy terrain where many boulders are scattered, and symmetry has dissolved. There he loses himself in a meandering and introverted zone with bent and zigzag stepped paths, leading to successive terraces. Then he finds his way up a long corridor between the rock and the mirror wall, and winds up north around the lion sculpture and the plateau. Originally, the mirror wall was continuous and high enough to hide his view of the plain below. This sequence thus focused the spectator's attention on the paintings.
It is only when the spectator reaches the summit of the rock that a 360° panorama suddenly appears and both the western and eastern gardens are revealed in their entirety. Here a new sequence unfolds, and a new relationship with the open landscape is evident.
In Sigiriya there is one preferential pathway, each sequence is treated by itself, without confusion and distraction from outside views. This has been achieved also with the use of thick vegetation now gone, and only on the plateau on top of the rock does one get a synthesis of the whole garden scheme.

Water Gardens

The water gardens are the most extensive and intricate ones and occupy the greater part of the western precinct. The measurements of the inner western precinct are 900 x 800 m. They feature five moated islands, two miniature gardens, reflecting pools, winding artificial streams, underground water systems and fountains, and extend from the western boundary of the Boulder Gardens to the Western ('Drawbridge') entrance and a double moat. The walled central garden consists of an artificial island surrounded by water and linked to the main precinct by cardinally oriented causeways, in a classic mandala plan, resembling the 'four garden' or *char bagh* concept of the Persian gardens (6th century BCE) and the Mughal garden design of a later period. However, unlike most *char baghs*, the four arms of the Sigiriya *char bagh* are water-filled and the garden formed by four causeways linked to a central island, on which there was a palace or roofed pavilion. On either side of the *char bagh*, that is on its eastern and western flanks, are further water-retaining structures shallow, marble-paved reflecting pools and deep wells.

This central area of the water garden also displays a form of 'echo planning' where the garden elements on one side of the central axial pathway are repeated in a mirror image on the other. At some distance from the central 'island' are two large 'moated islands', one to the north and the other to the south of the central *char bagh*. On a very different scale are two miniature gardens. One of these has been excavated and the other left for future investigation using non-intrusive techniques.

The overall plan of the Sigiriya moats and water gardens recalls, in concept if not in scale, many other Asian city and temple planning and garden traditions, such as at Angkor in Cambodia, Mughal gardens in India and Pakistan and the Forbidden City in Beijing, all of which Sigiriya predates.

Left:
The central *char bagh* of the water garden with the miniature gardens in the foreground.

Right:
The western entrance and beginning of the axial main walkway.

Previous page, top:
Parts of the water garden; in the foreground a detail of the miniature garden. The U-form surrounding what was probably a pavilion was a reflecting pool with a polished limestone pavement and very little water!

Previous page, bottom:
The axial main way is flanked on both sides by oblong pools.
Photocomposition: Ivan Baranowski, Zurich

Details of the water garden. The aerial photo shows the *char bagh* at the top, one of the moated islands to the left and beside the axial main walkway this organic exception to the overall geometric design, like a river. Note also the lower photo on the right.

Boulder Gardens

A widespread phenomenon in Asia is the location of shrines or settlements at what are often called cave sites, usually in a mountainous region, with an appropriate natural topography. An integral element of these rock shelters is the organisation of garden space. The boulder garden complex is in marked contrast to the symmetry and geometry of the water gardens. It is an entirely organic or asymmetrical composition consisting of a number of winding pathways and flights of stone stairs linking several clusters of large natural boulders extending across the western and northern slopes of the hill around the rock. As cut marks on the boulders and other archaeological remains indicate, buildings or pavilions with brick and timber superstructures and tiled roofs were erected on the summits of the boulders. A greater part of the natural form of the rock was left exposed, while rock-shelters with lean-to roofs were erected around the bases of the boulders. In their total design, therefore, the boulder gardens present an extraordinary architectural and garden landscape, whose principal characteristic is a series of rock clusters with tiled roof buildings on them and 'cave' pavilions below, all elaborately decorated and painted, and linked by pathways and flights of steps now badly weathered but originally of polished marble (crystalline limestone).

This octagonal pool at the end of the water garden meets the boulder landscape at the foot of the central rock.

Climbing up to the rock through the dramatic variety of boulder configurations is exciting.

After climbing through the boulders, the terrain becomes steeper and had been terraced by high retaining walls. These are the terrace gardens. Long steep stairways allow the visitor to get ever closer to the rock, and finally to reach the Lion Staircase terrace.

Terrace Gardens

Overlapping the boulder gardens is the third garden form at Sigiriya, the Terrace Gardens. These have been formed mostly by the construction of a series of rubble retaining walls, each rising above the other, exploiting the natural topography and running in a roughly concentric plan encircling the rock. There is no clear boundary between the two garden types, the one merging into the other. The terrace gardens seem to have had little or no architectural features rendered in brick or stone, except retaining walls and stairways linking terraces. This created a network of pathways through the boulder strewn hillsides that surround the rock. Two staircases on the eastern side of the rock, and one from the southwest, traverse the Boulder Gardens and converge on the Lion Staircase terrace, the highest and ultimate terrace with a 180° view over the surrounding landscape.

On the northern face of the rock, the Lion terrace is the base of the sculptured lion monumental staircase, 14 m high, which gave access to the royal palace on the summit.

The Lion Staircase and the Summit

The Lion was in effect the solitary and ultimate gatehouse to the palace on the summit. One of Sigiriya's most dramatic features is the great Lion staircase, now preserved only in the shape of two colossal paws and a mass of brick masonry surrounding the ancient limestone steps. The Lion, so impressive even in its ruined state today, must have afforded a vision of grandeur and majesty when it was intact. The staircase house reached a height of 14 m. Above this, the sloping rockface was utilised again to erect a gently ascending gallery and staircase of brick masonry with stone risers.

The 1.5 ha summit is the site of the main palace. It consists of a series of terraces of varying widths and heights, hosting a complex of architecture, gardens, and several water-retaining structures. A combination of the three basic garden types is centred on a massive rock-cut pool, which is supplemented by a number of smaller water-retaining structures, ensuring the sustainability of the human occupation and the floral complex of 'the garden in the sky'. The summit is not only the highest but also

The highest terraces were the basis of the palace, which must have been a wooden structure. On the lower level are the terraced structures of the palace gardens, at their centre a massive rock-cut pool.

Top left:
One of the two preserved colossal paws allows the visitor to imagine the grandeur of the lion.

Top right:
The palace garden terraces.

Bottom:
The pool and the splendid view.

View from the summit westwards over the water gardens and the axial main walkway, in the direction of a distant modern statue of the Buddha.

View of the eastern part of the water gardens with the octagonal pool and the huge boulder to the right.

the centre point of the axial median running east-west through the middle of the water gardens, on one side of the rock, and the north-south axis through the inner and outer cities, on the other. The axes converge at the centre point of the summit to form the basis of the modular grid covering the entire site and its periphery. Much of the architectural layout of the royal city and its moats and pools is controlled by this grid which traverses the site in the four cardinal directions. Walled precincts, gatehouses, various water-retaining structures, deep wells, underground water conduits, fountains, artificial streams, and moated islands combine to adjust structural symmetries to the natural topography.

This marriage of symmetry and asymmetry is epitomised by the *Octagonal Pool*, a special brick-built and stone-lined feature constructed around a massive boulder on a commanding position over the water gardens. This simple but brilliant combination of social

imperatives, natural topography and planning mathematics is also a clear display of one of the frequent guiding principles of Sri Lankan garden design, the *vista,* or landscape view. The grandest vista Sigiriya has to offer is the near-360-degree view of the horizon rim of distant mountains. The visual panorama thus conceptually defines the scope and authority of the Sigiriya's grand aesthetic and political statement.

Sigiriya was a large-scale territorial project, and at the same time there was a subtle attention to detail at a small scale. For the boulder- and terrace gardens the tradition and experience of the monastic gardens were essential. But what about the pleasure and water gardens? Without a doubt, at that period the Singhalese had the technical know-how to realise such a sophisticated water management system. But what was their source of inspiration? From where came their ideas? Who were the builders? The answers to these questions are still now a mystery.

Sigiriya, an excavated garden ruin, or a skeleton, has become today a park with its own aesthetic, replete with motifs of its own, such as the many brick walls covered with algae and moss. The ancient gardens have become a new park with its own beauty stimulating the imagination. One discovers not only what is physically there, but also what our imagination sees behind or beneath this reality.

The trees play a major role in this. Very little is known of the original tree planting and vegetation. After the passage of centuries, remains of dead trees are no longer to be found in the ground. Prior to the excavations began, the field of ruins was almost completely overgrown with jungle, just as the unexcavated parts of the park still are today. Archaeologists first had to clear the ground and then remove a thick layer of earth and humus. In the process, they left individual or groups of trees standing, more or less at random. Almost all of them stand on small hills, thus revealing the height of the layer of earth removed by the archaeologists. In this way, the archaeologists unintentionally became garden designers. The special park-like atmosphere with its light and shadows is very much appreciated by today's visitors.

An example of trees predating the archaeological intervention; the trees are preserved on small mounds, which is quite a common feature of archaeological sites.

Polonnaruwa

In contrast to the well preserved and clearly understandable morphology of the Sigiriya and Anuradhapura gardens we have the fragmentary and enigmatic remains of a 12th-century royal garden at Polonnaruwa, commissioned by Parakramabahu I (1154-86). Considered by many historians to be the most powerful figure in Sri Lankan history, it was he who presided over the apogee of the classic period of Sri Lanka's history and culture during the latter half of the 12th century. After a complex series of political and military actions he established his hegemony over the entire country with his capital at Polonnaruwa, already a major political centre.

We may interpret as an index of the wealth of this period the *Mahāvaṃsa* record of over thirty named gardens and several parks commissioned by Parakramabahu.[1] Although part of a grand, multi-period epic in elegant Pali poetry, these entries in the chronicle record can be read as a reliable, straightforward record-keeper's list. This part of the *Mahāvaṃsa* was composed in the early 13th century,[2] only a few decades after the end of Parakramabahu's reign and is almost certainly based on contemporary sources. A single stanza sums up his achievement:

> By constructing in this way beautiful viharas, gardens, tanks and the like he adorned with these numerous [works] the whole of Lanka.[3]

The sequence 'viharas, gardens, tanks and the like' is significant; it can be taken as an indicator of the social and ideological ranking attached to gardens. The description of the king's private garden, the Nandana-uyana and the associated garden for 'the community', the Lakkhuyyana, is spread over fourteen stanzas (*Mv* 79:1-12, 20, 22) and starts with a particularly significant record:

> As the King wished to make all articles (of food) needed by the townspeople easily attainable, he laid out gardens at different places. He who was the delight of his subjects, laid out the garden called Nandana which was adorned with hundreds of trees bearing fruit and blossom. The King planted coco palms, mango, and bread-fruit trees, areka and Palmyra palms and other trees, a hundred thousand of each kind and laid out in this way with great pains a large garden destined for the community which, because the name was appropriate, was known generally as the Lakkhuyyana. For the bathing of the bhikkhus in the hot season he had two charming ponds made there beneath hollow rocks.[4]

As we have seen, the most detailed description of a garden in the *Mahāvaṃsa* is contained in the series of verses on the Nandana-uyana[5] and the associated Dipuyyana and various pools and ponds (*Mv* 73: 95-123). Stripped of literary ornament, the image we have of this complex is a rare, and presumably 'realistic', record of an Asian royal garden from classic times, by a contemporary chronicler. Archaeologists and historians generally locate the 'Nandana-uyana' near the Nissanka Malla Audience Hall and Council Chamber palace complex. Incomprehensibly, little attention has been paid to find or investigate any traces of these gardens. While the gardens at Sigiriya and the Ranmasu Uyana in Anuradhapura are immediately readable as the skeletons of garden designs of great complexity and subtlety on a relatively large scale, the archaeological remains at Polonnaruwa need interpretation as they are not easily identifiable on the ground (see *Mv* 16ff; 78: 95-123). However, the creativity and vision of the Polonnaruwa architects, so impressively embodied in their monumental works, are also present in fragments of their gardens which, when put together, provide a somewhat different story. This need of interpretation is now on the way to be accomplished. On 3 August 2024 a team of archaeologists from Kelaniya University and La Trobe University Australia announced

At Polonnaruwa several kinds of beautiful pools have been found, but their historical context has been little investigated. From left to right: Kumara pokuna, a classic mandala; a highly elaborate swastika pokuna; the Lotus pool is a masterpiece of stonework.

The Parakrama Samudra, the largest lake at a royal capital in Sri Lanka. In the foreground the long, man-made earth dam, 12th century; in the background, the Dipa Uyana peninsula.

Top:
A detailed view of the peninsula, with the 19th-century resthouse on the promontory, and to the right the ruins of the royal garden.

Bottom:
The ruins of the royal Audience Hall and the Council Chamber surrounded by the garden, and the nearest of the three islands.

that their LIDAR-assisted survey (laser imaging detection and ranging) at Polonnaruwa, revealed the existence, under the rubble, of a hidden garden, similar to the Sigiriya's, within the walled ancient city. It contains four interconnected ponds, well-planned paths and intricate waterways, enclosed by a brick wall. Sri Lanka's garden history is still open for new discoveries!

What is today popularly known at Polonnaruwa today as garden remains are the water palaces, several stone lined pools in little-investigated contexts within the area of the walled city, and the enigmatic remains of the baths of Nissanka Malla. The little recognised icons of the ancient architects work should surely include the beautiful stone lotus pools and the classic mandala of the Kumara pokuna and of course the intrinsic garden landscapes of the ruined monasteries themselves. Not unlike the situation at Anuradhapura, where the only visible surviving garden remains are those of the Ranmasu Uyana below the dam of the Tissawava (the city lake), the only significant garden remains at Polonnaruwa still visible today stand on the shores of what is the largest lake at a royal capital in Sri Lanka, the Parakrama Samudra. These inner city and palace complexes certainly made the most of their situation on the lakeshore, not only in terms of utility, but also for the purposes of beauty and pleasure. Seen from a distance across the water, the citadel must have been the crowning glory of the lake, while viewed from the citadel ramparts or the higher buildings inside the walled city the entire expanse of the lake provided a permanent spectacle of landscape and light.

The action of the master designers stepping outside the city ramparts to a peninsula, or an island nearby seems to have been a conscious decision to further exploit this beauty, and to put on prominent display both private and public royal buildings in a new way. The major island or, in fact, peninsula, reaching out into the lake next to the city, was dominated by the royal Audience Hall and the Council Chamber of Nissanka (1189-1196). Three other small islets, one of them in the middle of the lake, and the other two on its borders, gave additional opportunities for smaller and more private water palaces or pavilions. We can now see that the ancient Dipuyyana or 'Garden of Islands', Parakrambahu's favourite 'daytime resort', was in fact a network of three islands visually linked to each other by the waters of the Parakrama Samudra:

A network of three pleasure islands in the Parakrama lake, reachable by boat from the main island, today a peninsula.

This view shows the pools no. 7 and 8 situated in the garden.

Previous page:
The three islands. On each of them are the ruins of pavilions and gardens.

Top:
The nearest island.

Centre:
The northernmost and largest one.

Bottom:
The smallest island in the middle of the lake.

> The Monarch also laid out the Dipuyyana resplendent in beauty which was to be glorified by his own continual presence during the day [...][6]

The water from the Parakrama Samudra was also used for a succession of baths and pokunas (5, 6, 7, 8). The ancient water management system involved an inlet sluice (9), an outlet sluice (10), and a low-level sluice (11) as identified by Bell in 1901.[7] The ancient status of the lower wet area between the peninsula (or promontory), and the foot of the citadel ramparts, is still unexplored. The south-western quadrant of the city is a meeting point of the main city wall, the ramparts of the citadel, the dam of the lake and the inlet and outlet sluices, and it is one of the key locations where one can observe the technological advances of the garden designers of Polonnaruwa. The conjectural explanations of the complex hydraulics illustrate this well. Concerning the development of the dams that make up the great lake, there are two possible hypotheses as illustrated: the first one states that the north-western lake dam is from the original period, the water flowing from the lake through sluice 9 with the system of the two pokunas converging in a secondary lake which occupied the whole actual lower wetland. This explains the function of the outlet sluice (10), which permits the overflow of this secondary lake into the main irrigation canal through the embankment connecting the peninsula with the citadel (see Inset box).[8] According to the second hypothesis, at least a part of the lower wetland was a garden, the Nandana Uyana, irrigated by the water coming through the system of the two pokunas, and probably supplying a network of canals and ponds, alternating with planted or cultivated areas. Sluice 10 was therefore the outlet of this water and gardens system.

The water palaces in the Sea of Parakrama and the elaborate technology involved in using the head of water from this lake to operate the royal baths and beautiful royal lotus pools give us some idea of the scope and character of the water gardens of Polonnaruwa.

Trough inlet sluice no. 9. Water from the Parakrama lake arrives first at pool no. 7, whose design is something quite unique.

Bottom right: Two small, highly sophisticated baths.

POLONNARUWA, DIPA UYANA

1 Council chamber
2 Audience Hall, Palace
3 Island Pavilion
4 Mausoleum
5 Baths
6 Baths
7 Pokunas, Pools
8 Pokunas, Pools
9 Inlet sluice
10 Outlet sluice
11 Main sluice
12 Hindu Temple
13 Dagoba
14 Today's Resthouse
15 Today's Museum
16 Rampart of the ancient Citadel

Source: «Polonnaruwa: Plan of Ruins on Promontory», Annual Report of the Archaeological Survey of Ceylon, 1901, H.C.P. Bell, adapted and completed, based on measurements on the site, by the author

A secondary lake surrounding the promontory?
A hypothesis

Notes from the author's investigations, February 2014 and February 2018

The aim of our investigations was to verify the hypothesis that the Dipauyana promontory was originally surrounded on the eastern side by a second lake on a lower level than the main lake. Bell's annual reports (*ASCAR*) of his activities on the site of Dipauyana in 1900, 1901 and 1909, published in the *Ceylon Sessional Papers* (1904, 1907, 1914), served as guide and inspiration for all our considerations.

Particular attention was given to the following aspects:

The arrival of the water in the pokunas

Regulated by the sluice no. 9, a perfect piece of engineering integrated in the dam, the water appears in the slope of the Parakrama dam, approximately 5 m lower than the dam's top, flowing

After passing the inlet sluice (above), a fishtail opening leads the water to fall in a great cascade into pool no. 7.

Next page, bottom:
From pool no. 7 the water has to pass a system of openings into pool no. 8, from where it enters at last into what we might call a secondary lake.

out of a well-designed stone-made triple opening like a source. It then flows through a stone channel, 6 -7 m long, spreading out like a fish-tail, until finishing in a perfectly designed, about 3 m large waterfall, arriving 1,20 m lower in the upper pokuna no. 7. The result is a masterpiece of scenic water design.

Pokunas no. 7 and no. 8

The level the pokunas were filled up with water is still difficult to evaluate. The maximum level could have been just under the large brick bank, running along the southern and eastern border of pokuna no. 7. The same applies to pokuna no. 8. Our initial impression was that the four openings in the crown of the separating wall between the two pokunas were the overflow from no. 7 to no. 8. This is indeed impossible, since the water level could not be higher than the waterfall, and the wall of no. 8 does not have such openings. In fact, the two conjunct pokunas are communicating through two or three openings in the basement of the separating wall, and the outflows on the east side of no. 8 have two similar openings in the basement of the wall. Hence the water level of the two pokunas was not higher than the brick bank, in both basins. We of course do not know whether the function of the pokunas was related to bathing, ritual washing, or water sports, or if they had rather a decorative role, with water lilies or lotus. The extraordinary architectural form of pokuna no.7 shows however that it contributed since the beginning to the beauty of the place.

The water coming from the Parakrama lake, which flows through the two pokunas, was evacuated from the lower pokuna by two openings in the wall basement into the lower land, which still function today. It is difficult to imagine the quantity of the original outflow. The only indication is the 3 m wide cascade, a noisy and splendid water curtain, which needed a considerable mass of water. Additional to this came the water running through the bathing pokunas no. 5 and no. 6 on the northern side.

The lower land between the promontory and the western citadel wall

There is a strong argument for our hypothesis of the secondary lower lake: even today (2014) the site behind the Museum and its parking is regularly flooded and becomes during the rainy seasons a pond. The Museum has been constructed on

Another example of a secondary lake exists on the north-eastern shore of the Parakrama lake. An impressive building for an ancient inlet sluice, integrated into the lake shore dam, sends water into a second lake about 2 m below and behind the dam.

the strip of land which separates the lower land from the main irrigation canal originating in the Parakrama lake. The Museum's parking has been filled up only recently. More northwards from the actual pond the lower region is still marshland, and temporarily flooded.

Outlet sluice no. 10

The only element of the water system we could not identify on site was the outlet sluice no. 10. Bell located it as the final sluice of the system, which gave back the water from the lower land to the main outflow of the Parakrama lake. It is the necessary complement to the inlet sluice no. 9. Bell reports the exact dimensions of this square construction: 5,80 x 5,80 m with a silt-well 2,40 x 2,40 m, 2,80 m deep, at its centre. Such an important and solid construction must have served a secondary lake, and not only some garden irrigation channels.

Unfortunately, the whole area where this sluice was situated suffered of large transformations related to the construction of the Museum. Outlet sluice no. 10 must have looked very similar to the sluice situated 2 km north from Dipauyana, in front of the northern one of the three islands. It is a massive ancient sluice on the lake shore, integrated in the dam, feeding a big secondary lake. The impression from the helicopter permitted us to situate the sluice. With 7,50 x 7,50 m and a well of 2,50 x 2,50 m in the middle its dimensions are quite impressive. The dam covered with trees separates the secondary lake, which has today a level around 2 m deeper than the main lake. The secondary lake extends itself to the boulder complex on the north-eastern side, near the Minneriya Road, with the ruins of an ancient Hindu Temple. This lake on a lower level and the Hindu Temple in the background

Top:
A pond, a fragment of what could have been the secondary lake, was still visible near the Museum in 2014.

Bottom and next page:
The perfectly square sluice building, 7.50 x 7.50 m, with a deep well in the middle.

were probably parts of a major well-designed scenery; it shows that there were not only one, but two secondary lakes at Polonnaruwa.

Bell's archaeological reports

With regards to the outflow the double pokunas and the lower land, Bell also mentions the probability of garden irrigation: 'How the water after leaving the two conjunct pokunas was utilized for irrigating the area outside of the *Kings Garden* is past ascertainment.' Bell mentions also irrigation channels, that is the 'historical *Nandana Uyana*' and 'the superfluous water of the Kings Garden'. (*ASCAR* 1901, p. 677) He was probably right in postulating that parts of the lower land between the promontory and the citadel wall were gardens, in combination with the lake. The *Mahavamsa*, cited by Bell (*ASCAR* 1901, p. 679), concerning the *Nandana Uyana*, the garden of heaven, is valuable in this regard: 'It was interspersed also with sheets of water ornamented with fine banks, and made pleasant by the abundant growth of the lotus and the lily, and the musical tones of the seras.' Only further archaeological investigations will be able to provide answers to these fascinating questions.

Between 2014 and 2018 the lower wetland, partly abandoned, and partly a grassland with a pond, was transformed into a modern public park with a lawn, a series of trees, decorative shrubs, and walkways. A small river or canal is the only remaining presence of water. The ancient unexplored structures have probably been destroyed forever.

Shifting Capitals

Stepping outside the framework of royal gardens there are significant exceptions to the hiatus in garden remains in the Late Historical Period (13th-early19th centuries). This applies particularly to the boulder-and-terrace garden complexes which had a continuous or near continuous history, not only in the Kandyan kingdom but also in the southern and western regions of the country, which came under colonial occupation from about the late 16th century onwards. Sites such as Dambulla in the Kandyan kingdom, Mulkirigala in the south and several Buddhist monasteries in the hinterland of Colombo, Galle and Matara are all places of great antiquity retaining the principal elements of their rock-shelter, boulder-and-terrace garden complexes through the vicissitudes of the post-classic era. They emerge in the 18th and 19th centuries as persistent survivals of ancient garden design, bearing the unmistakable signs of the various periods of their multi-layered histories. They give us the opportunity to study in a living form archetypal Sri Lankan garden types that have lasted over centuries.

Although we only have a limited body of evidence, the rare survivals of royal gardens at the boundaries of the hiatus bear witness to the continuing application of some of the key elements of garden design. The memory of the garden traditions of the classic era of the Early and Middle Historical periods seems to have been retained over the time gap of five centuries between Polonnaruwa and Kandy. Although there has been little archaeological focus on identifying and retrieving material from the hiatus, by following the

trajectory of this development we may extrapolate some of the continuities that allow us to propose an outline history of royal gardens in Sri Lanka.

The lost creations of the architects of the post-Polonnaruwa epoch at sites such as Yapahuva, Kurunegala and Kotte may not have matched that of their predecessors, but they exhibit a rich potential for garden archaeology. At Yapahuva we see one of the grandest staircases in Sri Lanka, leading to a sequence of natural rock terrace sites for what is thought to have been a palace and Tooth Relic temple complex, and a double arc of moats extending over a kilometre at its widest. Kurunegala has a lake, fragments of carved stone found at a lakeside site, and traces of city walls around a vast expanse of exposed bedrock. Kotte, probably the largest fortified urban centre in Sri Lanka in historical times, is located on a triangular site surrounded by marshes.

The scant remains of these late period royal and urban centres display the various periods of their multi-layered histories, and often give us the opportunity to study in a living form archetypal Sri Lankan garden types that have endured over the centuries. In these urban plans we can sense artistic sensibilities as distinctive as those that are to be seen in earlier times, and a grand vision of landscape whose development resurfaces in Kandy.

Kandy

The historical tradition reaches its final expression in the grand designed landscapes of the regions surrounding and including the royal city of Senkadagala, or Kandy, its English name. The last of Sri Lanka's royal cities and a World Heritage site, it is a living example of a designed urban royal landscape of the 18th and 19th centuries, whose basic structure and form are still preserved. The city and its southern suburb of Peradeniya have been closely associated with the history of the country and with royal gardens over a period of several centuries. Founded as early as the 15th century, the mountain kingdom became the central repository of Sri Lankan culture and civilisation during the Portuguese and Dutch occupations of the maritime regions in the 17th and 18th centuries. The surrender of Kandy in 1815 marks the colonial occupation of the entire country, lasting for a period of nearly one-and-half centuries.

The old city is located on one side of a wide, elevated valley floor flanked on east and west (and also some distance away on the south) by steep mountain ranges originally covered with dense forest. At some distance from Kandy itself the mountain terrain creates two sharp bends in the country's longest river, the Mahavali. Cradled in the smaller of these two bends – both taking the form of 'riverine peninsulas' – is Peradeniya, the location of a royal garden earlier than Kandy itself. Peradeniya was originally a royal retreat and even briefly a royal residence, first in the latter part of the 14th century, and again much later in the 18th century.

The city of Kandy as we know it today was established as a royal capital during the time of Narendrasinha (1707-1739) whose long reign spanned the first four decades of the 18th century. In its present form the city is much more than a footnote in Sri Lanka's historic garden traditions. One of the few surviving examples of a living premodern urban complex greatly modified in recent decades and much obliterated by modern accretions, it still retains some of the essential aspects of its historic morphology and landscape including temples and the scant remains of other traditional monuments.

The principal elements of the landscape are the moated ritual and royal centre, the historic street grid of the old inner city, the lake with its water palaces and the surrounding mountains. The moated ritual and royal centre – of royal palace, Tooth-Relic temple, and shrines dedicated to protective deities – is surrounded on three sides by the extensive Kandy Lake, a public square in front of the palace, and the grid-planned streets of the adjacent urban centre. In addition, an urban forest garden containing royal bathing pools was associated with the palace zone along the Udawattakale hill ranges, from the early days.

Presiding over the public square is the *Octagon* (Pattiruppuva), a unique version of an architectural form in Sri Lanka associated exclusively with royal contexts. The *Octagon* and the royal complex contain the innermost shrine of the Temple of the Tooth-Relic (one of the best surviving examples of traditional Sri Lankan architecture in the classic timber-and-masonry style), the royal Audience Hall, a section of the main palace and several other smaller courtyard palaces. Despite an over-arching background of multi-storeyed modern additions in a neo-Kandyan style, the iconic form of the *Octagon* stands out. This was one of the last major buildings to be added to the palace complex before the British occupation in 1815. It is a curious phenomenon, surely more than a coincidence, that unusual features such as island palaces and octagonal structures should occur almost exclusively in royal contexts. Elsewhere in the country water palaces are found only in the garden remains at Sigiriya, Anuradhapura and Polonnaruwa.

This tradition of water palaces and octagonal structures continues as a feature of royal gardens over a period of twelve centuries. It is possible that the Sri Lankan master builders of the 18th century had studied royal gardens at earlier sites. This is not too farfetched a notion as we have a precedent in the Kandyan painters at Dambulla in the 18th century studying and

One of the shifting capitals during the post-Polonnaruwa epoch was Yapahuwa (15th century). A powerful rock, similar to the Sigiriya rock, was the centre and at its foot was the walled and moated city. A monumental staircase, the grandest in Sri Lanka, leads up to a natural rock terrace, site of a palace and a temple. The last sequence, accompanied by beautiful sculptures, reaches an elaborate gatehouse from where the view is magnificent.

A view over the city of Kandy at the end of the 19th century. *Photo courtesy of a restaurant in the old city of Kandy. Photographer unknown.*

reinterpreting the 5th century paintings at Sigiriya executed twelve hundred years earlier.[9] The association of the water palaces with the building complexes surrounding the Tooth Relic Temple, the Audience Hall and the royal council chamber, would then lend support to the identification of two royal gardens in Polonnaruwa, the Garden of Islands (Dipuyyana) and the Nandana Uyana described in the Chronicle. Important elements in the ritual centre are the shrines to the deities protecting the sacred relic, the royal palace, an (unfinished?) moat and an elaborate vaulted entrance pavilion.

The central feature of the city plan is a masterpiece of what we today call landscape architecture, the swansong of premodern Sri Lankan garden design. The largest core component of the new design was the splendid water-garden; an upper-lake *Kirimuhuda* the cosmic Sea of Milk, separated by a north-south aligned bund from the lower Bogambara Weva, a second lake: and the ensemble with tree borders and ornamental parapet wall, the lace-like design of the cloud wall, above which floats the palace complex. A rectangular island, the *Kundasale*, in the centre of the main lake was adorned with shade trees, flower beds and a pleasure pavilion, and reached by means of a folding bridge. The two-storey *Ulpange* (water palace) was close to the palace of the queens and contained an indoor pool, the Queen's Bath. In addition, there was a promenade forming a forecourt to the citadel and a park on the far side of the lake. The lost inner moats or water bodies with walls and bridges were a second dramatic feature of the waterscapes of Senkadagala. The vast sheets of water in the twin lakes and smaller moats attest to the fact that water in one form or another was a *sine qua non* of urban design.

Adjacent to the palace square, at its north-eastern corner, is the old residential street grid which once contained the residences of the feudal nobility, royal officials and other city dwellers. This grid dates back to the18th century. It is one of the few surviving examples of Sri Lankan inner urban planning going back to the vestigial street grid in the ancient city of Anuradhapura, where early urbanism first manifests itself around the mid-1st millennium BCE. The Kandy inner city contained the city residences of the Kandyan nobility and officials. Archival records, plans and elements of the surviving fabric show an extremely well-organised network of elite urban housing, with extensive internal courtyards and rear gardens, fronting directly onto the street grid. A rectangular, walled, formally planted king's garden is visible in the German draftsman Johann Heydt's plan of Kandy from 1763.

This settlement pattern provides important historical data for the study of premodern urbanism in Sri Lanka, and for the role of courtyard gardens in urban housing. Only the shadow of this urban landscape survives in the vestigial remains of less than twenty mansions (*valavvas*).

The greater part of the present urban fabric is a crowded, commercial high-street architecture dating from the late 19th and early 20th centuries, following the broad pattern of the earlier street houses. A considerable degree of modern rebuilding has changed the historical character of this entire area, but – at least until recent times – it was possible to see the skeletons and shadows of domestic urban gardens, a subject on which textual and archaeological records are almost entirely silent.

An alternative suburban system of domestic gardens is also noted in an account of the road from Kandy to Peradeniya: 'From Kandy to the Royal Botanic Garden at Peradeniya, the road for nearly four miles passes through a continuous suburb, in which almost every house is surrounded by a little garden of coco-nut palms, bread-fruit, and coffee-trees.'[10] This form of 'cottage', 'mansion' or 'villa' garden came to dominate urban and suburban housing in Sri Lanka in the 19th and 20th centuries and has its roots in Sri Lanka's rural Wet Zone peasant housing. In the absence of excavated remains of any significance ethno-archaeological investigations are the only source of information.

Peradeniya itself harks back to the early history of the royal residence and gardens of the Kandyan kings. It seems clear that a historic garden and residence of the rulers of the mountain kingdom had been in existence here over a long period of time. We have no idea, however, what form it took and at which precise location, but it is safe to assume that the royal garden was within the highly appropriate terrain, soil and water resources of the riverine peninsula which came to be called Peradeniya over the years. Peradeniya first appears in the historical record during the reign of Vikramababu III (1357-1374) of Gampola.[11]

Four centuries later, in the time of King Kirti Sri Rajasingha (1747-1781), Peradeniya is referred to once again as the location of a royal garden, while during the reign of his successor, the scholar-king Rajadhi Rajasinha (1781-1798), it is identified as the site of a royal residence.[12] Ironically, the building and gardens at Peradeniya, whatever their location and character, were destroyed, first by a British invading force in 1803, then restored but only to be demolished again in 1820 (see also 'Botanical Gardens' in the 'Colonial Encounter' chapter, p. 177).

From an archaeological perspective Peradeniya offers a unique opportunity to study the historical succession of an Asian garden complex from premodern to modern times. Non-intrusive sub-surface archaeological investigations might possibly retrieve at least some material evidence regarding the history and character of these early garden sites at Peradeniya.

Despite its rich garden traditions Sri Lankan art has nothing like the exquisite and highly informative art of the Persian and Indian miniature to give us a vivid experience of the way in which a royal garden was used. However, the murals of the Kandy period and of the 19th century contain many representations of natural features and garden elements – such as trees, flowers, water bodies, mountains – but in the stylised representational modes characteristic of Late Period art.

Two paintings stand out as records of interest to garden historians. The first of these is in the Danakirigala Rajamahavihara near Kandy. It dates from the latter half of the 18th century and is a depiction of a named royal garden, the Dasvatta, whose principal function, as its name indicates, was to provide 1000 flowers daily to the temple as a royal offering. The other is the grand ceiling painting of a sacred, cosmographic landscape displaying a combination of natural, stylised, and imagined features in a more than 10m long tour de force at Panadura. We may compare these images with Heydt's mid-18th century engraving of the walled garden of the royal palace.

The organisation of garden space often plays a fundamental role in the formation of the urban environment. Kandy is an ideal historical example. The 'wave wall' around the lake – itself a masterpiece of landscape design created by the damming of several small streams – turns a modest valley into a lake while the wave wall turns the lakeside temples and palaces into celestial regions.

The core of the old city illustrates well the political conflict between the Kandyan state and the invading and occupying force. The historic centre contains a number of period buildings from British times, including the Law Courts and St. Paul's Church. The British adopted a deliberate policy of occupying and dominating, both administratively and architecturally, the politico-religious centre of the Kandyan kingdom. The main palace was turned into the residence of the British Government Agent, the Law Courts were built above the Tooth Relic Temple, and the church with its tall neo-Gothic tower, attempted to dwarf the *devalas* and dominate the sacred square. To the east of the square, and overlooking the inner city, was built a neo-Classical 'palace' with landscaped gardens as a residence for the British Governor. However, despite this attempt to occupy and dominate the central architectural landscape of the capital, the strong lines of Kandyan urban planning and the distinctive royal and religious architecture have retained their authority over this urban space, its key component being the palace-temple-lake-mountain complex.

Today as in the past, this area forms the core of the historic city, with (a) the Temple of the Tooth; (b) several buildings, which are the remains of the royal palace complex; and (c) the sacred square containing three of the four *devala* dedicated to the gods. Prominent buildings in the palace complex are the old palace itself, the Audience Hall, a 'water palace' on the edge of the lake, incorporating the Queen's Bath, and an unfinished moat. Apart from these monuments, the area also contains several period buildings from British times.

The city centre of Kandy on the urban lake shore. The lace-like design of the parapet wall, inspired by clouds, is a masterpiece of urban aesthetics.

Top left:
The royal palace and Temple of the Tooth complex is situated between the foot of the Udawattakale hill (royal hunting forest) and the lake. The building on the lake shore is the Queen's Bath.

Top right:
The access to the Temple of the Tooth-Relic leads through an old public park, focusing on the Octagon.

Bottom left:
The lake and the surrounding landscape seen from the Udawattakele hill.

Bottom right:
The royal Audience Hall.

Left:
The lake-side promenade with the parapet wall; the island; the Ulpange (water palace) or Queen's Bath with an indoor pool.

Right:
A moat separates the Octagon and Temple front from the public park.

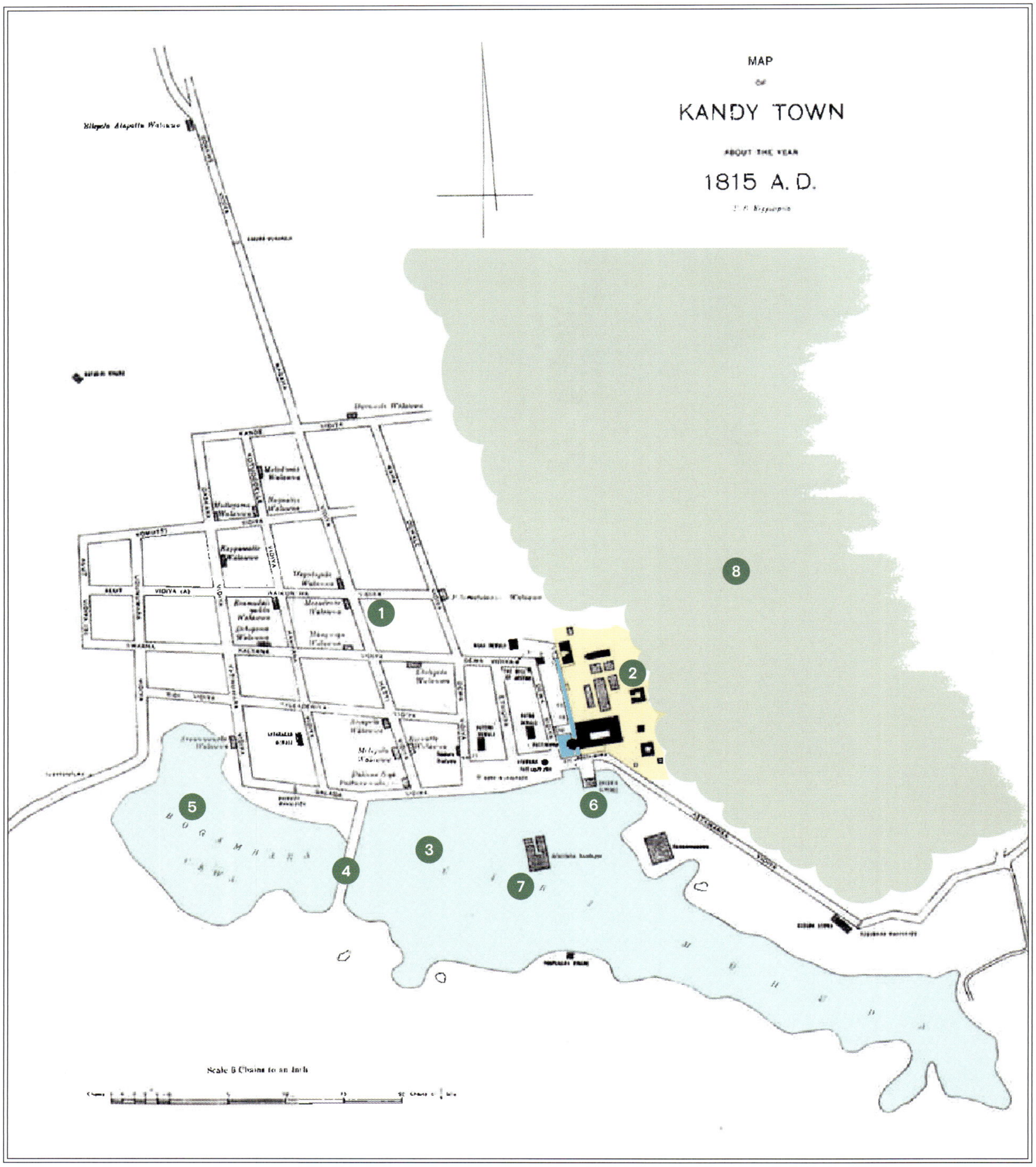

KANDY, Plan of the city in 1815

1. The Royal City of Kandy
2. The Temple of the tooth and Palace complex, protected by a moat
3. The Kiri Muhuda lake
4. The Dam between the two lakes
5. The Bogambara Vewa, no longer exists today
6. The Queen's bath house
7. A Pavilion and garden island
8. Royal Hunting forest, today a public park

Source: Reproduction from 'Kandy, an illustrated survey of ancient monuments, including maps of the city', edited by the Central Cultural Fund 1983, adapted by the author

This 18th-century wall painting in the Danakirigala temple depicts a royal garden, the Daswatta, whose function was to provide 1,000 flowers daily to the temple as a royal offering. The upper photo is from 2024; the lower one is a reproduction from Senake Bandaranayake's book on the wall paintings of Sri Lanka published in 1986 and shows the difference in the state of conservation.

1 This recalls the reference to Kasyapa's setting up of mango groves around the country nearly 600 years earlier.

2 The *Mahāvaṃsa* chronicles the history of Sri Lanka from its legendary beginnings to the reign of Kirti Sri Rajasinha (1788-1815). It is a continuous narrative in 100 chapters but consists of four parts composed at different periods of time: (1) The first section ends in the 51st stanza of Chapter 37, with reign of Mahasen in 302 BCE, and was written by Mahanama, a monk-scholar and poet, at the beginning of the 6th century BCE from earlier written and, probably, oral sources; (2) The second part, starting with the 51st stanza of Chapter 37, was compiled by Dharmakirti in the early years of the 13th century. It is particularly interesting to garden historians for the important position it gives to gardens in the culture of its times, the colourful description of the royal Nandana-uyana in Polonnaruwa and the extensive listing of gardens commissioned by Parakramabahu I; (3) The author of the third part is unknown, but it continues with the narrative and ends with the reign of Parakramabahu VI.

3 *Mv* 79: 85.

4 *Mv* 79: 6.

5 The Nandana uyana is named after the garden of Indra, the god presiding over the Svargaloka, a heaven to the north of Mount Meru. The garden in Polonnaruwa is not to be confused with the Nandana grove (Nandanavana) in Anuradhapura.

6 *Mv* 79: 6-7.

7 ASCAR 1901, 11 ff.

8 See ASCAR 1901, 11ff.

9 Bandaranayake/Jayasinghe 1986, 29, 157.

10 Tennent 1859, 207.

11 UCHC 1(2), 644.

12 Dewaraja 1972, 133.

Entrance and stone stairway leading to the renowned colossal Sasseruwa Buddha statue, which is part of the Rasvehera complex, one of the Giri monasteries. The statue is an unfinished high-relief, carved out of a large cliff, 13 m high and dating to the 8th century.

Monastic Gardens

Shanti Jayawardene
Klaus Holzhausen

Introduction

Archaeological remains of monastic gardens in Sri Lanka present truly astonishing scenarios of aesthetic elegance as well as of complex religious and social organisation. A variety of innovative forms are especially noticeable between the 5th and 12th centuries. However, connections between variations in these built forms and shifting patterns of religious doctrine and practice on the one hand, as well as social and political organisation on the other, are not yet well understood.

In Sri Lanka, the monastic order and the state came together in the Asokan model of kingship, a mode widely dispersed and legitimised in Asia from around 250 BCE onwards. Ascetic practices, drawing upon older indigenous and Indian lifestyles of renunciation[1] also gave rise to a tradition whereby Buddhist monks dwelt in rock-shelters in the wilderness. Over one thousand such rock-shelters – dating from between the 3rd century BCE and the 1st century CE – have been identified by donatory records, usually inscribed above the rock-shelter drip ledges.

Two archetypal monastic forms emerged at this time. Rock-shelters in the wilderness multiplied through the patronage of kings, nobles, merchants, craftsmen, Brahmans and others, and became the archetypal *giri* (hill) monasteries, some having remained in intermittent or continuous occupation to this day. The second monastic type is that of 'park' monasteries, or *arama* (or *vihāra*): set in parks or groves, they appeared in or around Anuradhapura, the country's principal royal capital, and also spread to other regions. Over a period of fifteen centuries or more this archetype, borrowing the accoutrements of secular urban parks, metamorphosed into several types of formally planned artificial sites, commanding large material resources. From the 1st century BCE onwards, monasteries were recipients of land grants, irrigation reservoirs and other forms of wealth, sometimes immune from state jurisdiction. Monastic overlords accumulated a rich independent treasury and developed a vast and complex administrative machinery to manage their extensive estates.

Anuradhapura

Dominating the subject of Sri Lankan monastic architecture is the city of Anuradhapura. As a royal and ritual hub it attracted pilgrims from all over the island and from other Buddhist regions of the world. The pilgrim circuit connected it to all the main religious centres in the country and it remained a city of some significance, at least until about the 13th century.

The architecture of the Anuradhapura monasteries has been studied in some detail by Sri Lanka's archaeologists. Their work offers a vision of how great wealth and client demand fashioned a monastic complex of a magisterial and sophisticated spatial order.[2] Nevertheless, emphasis on monuments as isolated objects has meant that landscapes and gardens in their widest sense have received little attention as subjects of study. The extent of monastic remains outside the city covers a land area more extensive than that within the city walls. Yet, the relationship between aristocracy and Sangha is still poorly understood; and its implications for the history of garden design remain obscure.

Of relevance to the subject of gardens is the increased investment in rich lifestyles reflected in the monastic landscapes of the Late Anuradhapura Period. The surface remains document how residential complexes competed with ritual precincts in size and design.[3] The gretaer investment in luxurious living leads us to expect a concomitantly greater investment in gardens between the 5th century with Sigiriya's royal grandeur and the end of the Anuradhapura epoch in the 10th century. It is in the succeeding Polonnaruwa Period that royal palaces on the scale of Sigiriya reappeared and stone started to be used for secular structures. In short, judging from the built forms in brick and stone throughout Sri Lanka's history, it seems that the greater material and intellectual investment in architecture and gardens took place in the monastery rather than in the palace, despite the magnificence of Sigiriya.[4] It was the expertise in water management and ecology acquired over many generations during the construction of countless reservoirs (*wewas* or tanks) as well as of complex irrigation systems that enabled the design of all the garden forms described below.

This is the Jetavana stupa at Anuradhapura in the middle of its square ceremonial terrace. Spatial conception and scale bear comparison with the pyramids of Gizeh in Egypt. The Jetavana was abandoned and has now been restored, but no longer has a ceremonial function.

Barring the little understood scale and spread of the agro-urban landscape incorporating monasteries, the most striking feature of the material remains at Anuradhapura is the giant scale of such ritual sites as the Abhayagiri or Jetavana stupa complex. Their high-walled gated compounds and terraces cover areas of 4.45 and 4 hectares respectively. Equally breath-taking are the towering stupas, between 90 and 120 metres in height, originally crowned with golden pinnacles. The same could be said of the spatial impact of other walled ritual precincts that contained fabled and fantastic multi-storeyed *uposathagharas* chapterhouses combining dwelling quarters, as well as *patimagharas* image houses. Ritual structures vied with the stupa, 'if not in size, then in architectural magnificence'.[5] The scale, spatial conception and gigantic human effort that went into erecting the stupa sites suggest an importance far surpassingthat of private devotion. A massive hemisphere, encircled by vast and walled geometric terraces, is evidence of pomp and temporal as well as cosmic power.

Historical chronicles recount how these monuments in spaces were used for secular and religious ceremonies involving thousands of people. They recreate unearthly scenes of stupa terraces transformed into colossal open-air stages drawing the heavens into their orbit. In the 2nd century CE, King Vasabah had a thousand lamps lit at the stupas in the Thuparama and Mahavihara.[6] During festivals the Mihintale stupa was covered with a red cloth and golden balls, as well as festooned with pearls; with chains of lamps along access paths, people were entertained with mime, songs, music, dancing and

The spaces and edifices were unquestionably symbolic as well as intended as sites for enacting grandiose spectacles, theatres for proclaiming the joint power of the state and Sangha. The imaginative energies enfolded therein attest to a long tradition of design. The largest of the sites is Abhayagiri, whose wealth, popularity and influence exceeded that of the Mahavihara, throughout almost the entire Anuradhapura era.

Landscape Aesthetic of 'Emptiness' or Restraint

The aesthetic of the stupa ritual space may paradoxically be described as one of emptiness, evoked by quite specific design attributes that include axial planning, flat terraces, stark geometrical shapes with little ornamentation, and the pronounced absence of plants and water. The symbiosis of right-angle and natural form appears common to most early garden traditions of West and East Asia.[9] In the ritual space of the stupa, architectural geometry shifts from the square and circle on plan to three-dimensional walled terraces and a central hemisphere: the cynosure. Could a spatial concept that balances elemental volumes, combined with a remarkable knowledge of proportion, have created the drama of this singular bare landscape or garden? The sense of entering a transcendental space was enhanced by axial paths or sightlines, diminutive architectural proportions and spatial links through devices such as gatehouses, stairways, altars, parapets and balustrades, along with simultaneous shifts of scale, vistas, floor levels and light and shade; not forgetting the primary use of bright, stark white[10] set against a sky whose predominantly blue colour kept changing. For the nobility, merchants, householders, craftsmen and peasants allowed to witness the display, usually staged on

drumming.[7] In the 5th century, the monks arranged themselves on the upper terrace of the Mahathupa in readiness to welcome a victorious king and his army. Indeed, the entry of the army into a sacred precinct testifies to the politico-religious significance of the site. Moreover, the vast terraces of Abhayagiri, for instance, accommodated around 30,000 people who participated in ceremonies to bathe the stupa with mechanical contrivances, or transformed it into a globe of scented flowers by pasting jasmines. On occasion the drains were plugged and the upper stone terrace transformed into a pool filled with perfumed oil on which to float lamps and lotuses.[8]

The Ruwanweli stupa or Ruwanweli Maha Seya in its completely white splendour is a venerated pilgrim centre where ceremonies are conducted daily and which are especially impressive at night. Only the human presence on the terrace shows its true scale and proportions.

moonlit nights, it must indeed have been experienced as an 'aesthetic shock',[11] and more.

The pre-eminence of the stupa declined after the 4th century, when the image cult became popular. The shift signals the growing appeal of Mahayana practice. Indoor rituals lacked the regal splendour afforded by sky and open space. Although elaborate ceremonies at monastic sites registered cultural interplay between kings, monks and the laity, archaeological accounts have yet to offer interpretations of the connections between these spaces, ritual functions and their designers' spatial imagination.[12] But we may ask whether it is this very interplay which suggests that monastic gardens embody a wealtgh of meanings connected as much with out-of-time spiritual imperatives as with temporal power and pleasures. Gardens, like all man-made sites, serve to reproduce certain social practices, which would of necessity elude us, unless gardens can be read as spaces intrinsic to and integrated with the ceremonial business of the wider landscape and its function in society.

Monastic architecture and gardens, then, were places and spaces where the symbiosis of court and Sangha was played out. They were sites of intellectual and material competition, articulating and reproducing relationships between the lifestyles of nobles or wealthy householders and those of monks. Their designs distil the worldly and spiritual spatial imagination of elite designers, free to roam the earth and celestial paradises, frequently summoned and so ornately detailed in the Buddhist *imaginaire*.[13] The sheer ingenuity and complexity of the material remains at these sites compel us to confront, if only in passing, the missing question of linking these traditions to wider concerns of aesthetics and power.

The massive and sophisticated corpus of Sanskrit literary culture that spread over a vast Asian geography and came to define a global cultural formation, anywhere between 300-1300 CE, has been named a 'cosmopolis'. It has been argued that this 'cosmopolis' transcended political and religious boundaries, 'uniting intellectuals and their masters in a common aesthetic culture'[14] in South and Southeast Asian polities. This culture served not only kings, but also an 'interpretive community' comprising a larger field of courtly culture which included Lanka's ruling elite. The rich emotional and aesthetic range of literary works, like the poems in the Sigiriya graffiti and the *Siyabaslakara*, offer rare insight into how deeply nature was embedded in the aesthetic culture of sections of the ruling class during the 8th to 10th centuries.[15]

The major monasteries of Anuradhapura were leading intellectual centres attracting scholars from all over the Buddhist world, including the renowned Indian savants Buddhagosa and Amarasimha. Chinese sources attest to the fact that the monks of Sri Lanka were 'distinguished for their powers of abstraction and their wisdom'.[16] We know nothing about the training received by those who designed monasteries and their gardens. It is likely that monastic intellectuals participated in architectural and garden design, especially since rituals and meditation have intimate associations with nature and forest environments. Indian and European experience demonstrates that secrecy was a key factor in the dissemination of design knowledge in the premodern world. Knowledge usually passed from master to disciple and was often jealously guarded by families or craft guilds. The consummate refinement of Sri Lanka's garden design traditions is concrete evidence that the designers' imagination was a valued commodity in the shared world of the dominant class. New research reveals that the powerful reach of the esoteric Buddhist masters of the *Pamsukilin* order attached to the Abhayagiri extended as far as China, Japan and Java. The monasteries of Java linked with Abhayagiri were, to some extent, physically modelled on Sri Lankan prototypes.[17]

Monastery Types

The monasteries of Sri Lanka have been classified into six categories, with numerous variants, according to a combination of site geography, architectural functions and plans.[18] The first two are the perennial organic versions of the *giri* monastery and various developments of the early *arama* or parkmonastery. The next category is the centric arrangement of the *arama* around a stupa or other ritual hub typical of the great metropolitan monasteries of Anuradhapura and Polonnaruwa. The *Pancayatana parivena* make up a range of monastic residences distinctive enough to form a category of their own.

The most widespread version of a monastery form in urban, suburban or rural contexts, the *pabbata vihara* appears in either highly formalised or organic variants. It consists essentially of a central ritual precinct surrounded or accompanied by monastic residences. The *padhanagara parivena* is a non-urban type which stands, often in clusters, in the wilderness.

Giri (Hill) Monasteries

Giri monasteries catered to a coenobitic lifestyle, adopted by Buddhist monks by the time Buddhism was officially endorsed in Sri Lanka. *Giri* monasteries are often called forest monasteries,[19] in which case the gardens are described as boulder gardens. Within a purely garden taxonomy they could belong to the hanging garden genre because they comprise a sequence of terraces hanging off the sides of mountains. By definition, this type is located on boulder-strewn hill slopes.

Varana temple and monastery is a typical example of a large rock shelter, protected from rainwater by a drip-ledge. Right: an example of a drip-ledge from Rajagirilenkanda.

They comprise partly excavated and natural rock-shelters with terraced floors, screen walls and lean-to roofs protected by drip-ledges cut into the rock. Entry is through doors in the wall. They are distinguished by the intrinsic design traits of multi-level organic plans, defined by the site topography. Inter alia, typical sites are the Rajagirilenkanda at Mihintale, the Sigiriya boulder garden and terrace garden rock-shelters and the monasteries at Dambulla, Bambaragala, Aluvihare and Kudumbigala. Several cave sites have distinctive inscribed names, including Pleasant Sight (*manapadasana*), Great View and Favourite View. The names bera witness to the depth of aesthetic appreciation of distant views which undoubtedly informed site selection.

Rajagirilenkanda, Mihintale

The abandoned Rajagirilena cave complex near Mihintale is an ancient *giri* monastery; although the architectural remains date from later phases of building, they bring us close to what such a monastery may have offered. Part excavated rock-shelters situated at different levels were linked by stairways zigzagging up and around the mountain. The floors of the shelters were level terraces of packed earth held by brick or stone revetments. Pools were a standard feature, either natural, part excavated or constructed. Drains cut into the rock diverted water from upper levels into pools near shelters. The terraces were connected by pathways lined with soft sand or compressed earth and steps cut into the rock or built. Ruins of freestanding ritual buildings and pools at ground level testify that over time rock-shelters became part of a more extensive establishment.

The first Commissioner of Archaeology in Ceylon, Harry Charles Purvis Bell's description of the Rajagirilena captures, in few words, the unfamiliar comfort and beauty of monastic cave life in Sri Lanka: 'A better hermitage for Buddhist monks could hardly be selected than these airy caverns. They provided every facility for quiet retreat within eight miles of Anuradhapura shrines, and were a far cry from the adjacent, yet wholly distinct monasteries at Mihintale and Anai Kutti Kanda. They command from their peaceful secluded elevation, unimpeded restful views across miles of dark green forest and silvery tanks.'[20]

Items such as the stupa and bodhi tree were introduced later into cave dwelling complexes and placed in separate walled terraces. They accommodated public worship and ritual functions. On occasion, the summits of several adjacent boulders were connected by flat bridging terraces to form larger precincts. The artificial terraces shared the contours of the hillside and transformed early cave sites into the archetypal hanging terraced gardens of the later *giri* monastery. The terraced gardens are the result of ritual art and architecture interwoven with geography and horticulture. They acquire format and flora from geography of place, with the aesthetic principle of restraint, while horticulture is mostly absent.

Left:
The Rajagirilenkanda rock-shelter complex seen from the south-west.

Top right:
Details of Rajagirilenkanda, one showing a pool.

Bottom right:
Very interesting is the visual relation with the Kaludiya Pokuna monastery and his lake, which is situated about 1 km away.

Over a span of 24 centuries, Mihintale developed into a complex site where several monastic types overlap, but the skeletal spatial layout of a *giri* monastery is still discernible. The so-called hospital site and some later residences survive at the lowest level. Here also begins the imposing avenue of steps that leads, via a formal gated entrance, to a large walled middle-level terrace. The middle terrace connects more walled precincts containing appurtenances such as the refectory (*uposathaghara*), pool and residential units. The stupa is often on the highest terrace.

Natural depressions on boulders are shaped into *kema pools* (there is no English equivalent) and incorporated into special pool-terraces. These man-made artificial rock pools are at times provided with ledges cut into the rock for seating. The appealing lion pool possesses a stone-carved rampant lion serving as a bathing spout; a giant hooded cobra guards a long pool: Naga

This great stairway is the main access to the hills of Mihintale. Its beauty lies in its generous simplicity and in the Frangipani trees (Plumeria alba, Temple tree) planted all along, on both sides. Mihintale is one of the most important pilgrimage sites in Sri Lanka, because it was here that Mahinda, who brought Buddhism from India in the 3rd century BCE, lived.

An overall view of Mihintale with the white landmark stupa on the hill top. In the foreground are the ruins of another stupa. The lines of light grey trees, quite different from forest trees, are the Frangipanis, planted along the pilgrim ways.

Pokuna. At times, several descending *kema* connected by hidden sluices are organised into beautiful cascades. The *kema* are deceptive both in size and in depth; their often small surface area, or narrow neck, balloons out horizontally and vertically into the boulders to reduce water evaporation in the dry season.[21] The views from the pool-terraces are exceptionally beautiful and draw in distant mountain, forest and skyscapes that attest to their intense aestheticisation.

A very spectacular example of a *kema* is Nuwaragala in the Eastern province, situated on a rock mountain above a cliff about 300 metres high, an 18 x 23,5 metres rectangular pool cut into the rock, so deep that you can swim. The view from this site is simply breathtaking. On the flat rock limiting the pool at the rear are traces of a former construction, probably a pavilion. The Nuwaragala site is yet to be excavated. H.C.P. Bell visited the place at the beginning of the 20th century.

Kema pools are frequent elements in Giri monasteries.

Top:
At Kudumbigala on the top of a giant boulder, the outlet of a natural hollow is closed by an earth dam to create a pool. The view from the pool over the wilderness, with the ocean on the horizon.

Middle:
Nuwaragala in the eastern province is an extraordinary archaeological site perched atop 200 m-high cliffs. The 18 x 24 m pool, cut into the rock, is so large that it is even visible on satellite images.

Bottom:
In Sri Lanka there are still hermits. A typical hermit cave, closed off by a yellow wall, in the Yala National Park. On the bare rock a very simple garden has been created by planting some Frangipani shrubs. The rock hill emerges from the jungle, opening onto a peaceful view.

Another element which can often been found in today's gardens near the caves still inhabited by hermit monks is the meditation path. It is a rectilinear, horizontal, sand-covered path, around 80 centimetres wide and 15 to 20 metres long. One end is mostly marked by a stone seat. This path (the *cankamana*) is used for open air walking meditation, going forwards and backwards.

Our present lack of archaeo-botanical knowledge renders it impossible to say whether horticulture featured in the design and, indeed, how the larger terraced gardens were designed. However, it is possible that the modern landscape of flat sand floors, with boulders that intermittently punctuate the level surface and large shade trees, harks back to a distant tradition of landscaping that evokes a faint sense of what they may have felt like a thousand years ago. Two examples serve to illustrate the actual state of Giri monasteries today.

At Kaludiya pokuna another hermit dwelling and its garden, with in the middle the typical cancamana, a clean sandy path for walking meditation.

The famous Dambulla Temple with its terrace and the *Bodhigara*, the Bodhi-tree. The pavement of the terrace is a recent addition to the original sand floor.

The Golden Temple at Dambulla

The first one is the Golden Temple (*Suvarnagiriguha*) at Dambulla. The most visible feature at Dambulla is the large rock over 160 metres in height. Around 80 rock-shelters in the surrounding area offered dwellings for monks in the past and some carry donatory inscriptions. Today, monks live in free-standing structures at ground level. Legend places its origins in I BCE. It was mentioned in the *Mahavamsa* in the 11th century reign of Vijayabahu I and later in the inscription of Nissankamalla in the 12th century.

Dambulla is famous for its five image-houses folded into the rock under a natural overhang almost at the summit. A large walled terrace garden gives access to this range of cave temples. The garden contains two rock pools and a Bodhi tree. In this case, the stupa is placed inside the image-house. The Dambulla terrace floor is part boulder and part paved (old photographs show pressed-earth and sand floors). It is not possible to say whether there was an original boundary wall. The garden affords magnificent views over the surrounding countryside and has all the basic ingredients of a typical terraced garden of a *giri* monastery. But due to its situation near a main road and not far from Sigiriya it became a popular tourist attraction and lost much of the innocence and simplicity of an original Giri monastery. Nevertheless, inside the cave temples many dignified statues and the overall wall- and ceiling paintings, all dating from the 18th century, create a very strong atmosphere. One particular painting presents an interesting garden landscape full of symbolic detail.

Inside the largest of the five image-houses one particular 18th-century wall painting illustrates a symbolic garden landscape. The cosmic lake Anotatta on top of the Mount Meru has an outlet at each cardinal direction in shape of the mouth of an animal. Many details are showing the importance of water in gardens. In the smaller photo the real situation is visible, with 2 seating Buddhas in front of it, preventing a complete view. A careful photocomposing work made it possible to see the complete painting without these statues. *Photocomposition: Ivan Baranowski, Zurich*

Situated in the north-eastern part of the Yala National Park on a colossal, high boulder formation, the Kudumbigala monastery enjoys a 360° view over the surrounding wilderness. In the centre a monk's dwelling is visible; the kema pool is to the left.
Photocomposition: Ivan Baranowski, Zurich

Kudumbigala

The second relevant example, found in Kudumbigala, south from Arugam Bay, in the Yala National Park, is still very authentic. According to Brahmi inscriptions, Kudumbigala was a monastery for ascetics. While we can date its inception to the 2nd century BCE, it has not been excavated. After being in the war zone for over 30 years, the site has experienced fitful occupation and is today still inhabited by some monks. It consists of a range of large boulder-strewn hills in a dry-zone jungle, constituting an almost unearthly sight. Several phases of building are evident. The first terrace is at middle level and has no walls. Set into it, at a slightly lower level, is an unusual tiny sand and boulder garden, bounded on one side by an extraordinary cluster of boulders into which is recessed an image-house. The remaining sides are bordered by a clumsy low stone wall of recent origin. A part of the boulder cluster intrudes on the floor of the lower section. Boulders are the dominant aesthetic feature of the terrace. From this terrace the path diverges: one path proceeds up the hill, and the other leads in the opposite direction, to a second range of hills on whose summit is a stupa.

The summit of the first hill contains ruins of the stupa, several pools, perhaps a water pavilion, and other

On a first terrace at the middle level, outside a boulder-cave image house, is a small, quite unique sand and boulder garden.

The summit of the boulder range is crowned by a ruined stupa.

Three kema pools on the large boulder area might be called a garden of pools.

buildings with stone columns and brick bases. An adjacent group of boulders forms the site of what can be identified as a garden of pools. The large boulders in this area have reasonably flat surfaces and contain three *kema* surrounded by crude recent parapets. A small, derelict modern pavilion, on a slightly higher boulder, may have served as a kind of viewing platform. Trees from the surrounding forest supply foliage for this otherwise bare rock and water garden. The absence of walls yields a rather unimpeded view over a dense green forest canopy to an aquamarine sea beyond. It is possible that these could amount to infinity pools when full. We have only to imagine a bather gazing at a gleaming sea, silvery and shimmering in the distance on a warm, moonlit tropical night.

The *kema* terrace is a distinctive garden component of *giri* monasteries. Sri Lankan expertise in the building of flat terraced gardens on hillsides or on large boulders, linked by winding paths, is most magnificently expressed at Sigiriya, which offers evidence that stairs and pathways were enclosed by roofs, walls and doorways. The pathways at Kudumbigala are unforgettable; they transport us into a silent unfamiliar world, part man-made and part wilderness. Paths are at times paved with rough stones or lined with soft white sand; low boulders and roots cross the floor at intervals. At places, the paths hug flowing boulders and dappled shade softens dark undulating surfaces; elsewhere, they weave through darker rocky defiles with gently sloping sides, always shaded by trees and vines in that light and intimate way characteristic of dry-zone flora. Punctuating the spatial intimacy are boulder-strewn

Covered with white sand or paved with stone steps, the pathways at Kudumbigala, which lead to the highest open space, provide an intimate atmosphere.

sunny open stretches offering intermittent views of sea, sky and forest. The contrast of white pathways, dark rock, blue sky and multiple forest greenery imperceptibly renders rapid shifts of space, light and shade, which are at once mysterious and pleasurable. The deep sense of solitude is occasionally interrupted by the call of birds and the wind soughing and swaying the trees. It is worth mentioning that the habits of watching the forest and the sea were ancient pastimes not only of monks but also of cultured elites and, possibly, of fisher folk and peasants too. The *Sandesas* poems, in which the poets invite us to share in their pleasure gained by a keen observation of nature, open a door to a fascinating lost world of joy in its contemplation.

> Be happy watching the forest flowers of the dawn
> Like the foam retained scattered on tree-tops
> When the water of moonlight filtered through
> Filling the world. *(Gira Sandesa)*
>
> Behold now, the great sea in the north
> With pearls, conches and corals glistening on its shore
> Where rows of waves swirled up by the wind
> Swell up towards the sky
> As if to embrace the lady, the Celestial River.[22]

Design Theories

It is indupitable that the mature *giri* monastery is a designed sacred landscape of forest, rock, water and views. The views of shimmering lakes and faraway mountain ranges shrouded in smoky cloud forests provide the distance and solitude to contemplate the insignificance of the self. *Giri* monasteries are testimony to a non-invasive aesthetic sensibility that regards the landscape as sacred. In spatio-conceptual domain and scale they are somewhat different to the elaborate rock-cut monasteries in India. They are small walled hanging-gardens whose designs anticipate the *karesansui* dry-landscapes of the Buddhist monastic gardens of 15th-century Japan. There is, however, a difference.

These gardens were built on mountain sites to harmonise with distant mountains, rivers and forests comprising an entire spiritual ecosystem. The morphology of the site was altered in such a way that any intervention would barely be visible. The appreciation of absence in the design ethos is striking. In the East Asian sand, boulder and water garden designs, the boulders and stones were brought from elsewhere and laid in a pre-planned arrangement at the chosen site. Hence these gardens are completely artificial. The *giri* monastery gardens are also almost completely artificial while appearing deceptively natural. The secular boulder-garden designs at Sigiriya are a particular Sri Lankan contribution to garden history.

Some ancient *giri* monasteries are living organisms that continue to cater to cave-dwelling monks, and their environments, too, may carry traces of earlier physical patterns. It is thus possible that the legacy of an older planting culture of empty or sparsely planted terrace gardens survives in the modern landscapes. Today, soft sand floors are swept in a variety of forms by special brooms, making the floor a veritable painting in motion. This austere elegance also combines the aesthetic attribute of emptiness – a design feature of the terraced garden normally overlooked by contemporary visitors. This is because it acquires a seamless naturalness from the way the retaining walls and sand and rock floors merge with the boulders already in place and borrow the rich vegetation of the forest. At times, only the boundary walls appear man-made. The constantly shifting chiaroscuro between jungle flora, shaded paths and bare un-shaded terrace is another typical design attribute.

The origins of the design theories inherent in the mature *giri* monastery gardens are yet to be reconstructed. It is too early to say whether the spare garden aesthetics noted here conforms to the equally austere architecture of the so-called meditation monasteries. Recent research connects the latter with the immensely powerful ascetic *Pamsukulin* sect known in the cosmopolitan Buddhist world as leading intellectuals and advanced meditation masters of the 'wilderness' tradition in Sri Lanka.[23]

Arama or Park Monasteries

Termed *arama*, these monasteries are mostly urban or semi-urban and situated on flat ground, usually located in a garden, park, or woodland. We may assume that they too were organic, with layouts governed by religious needs, resources available and site topography. As the monasteries from the earliest periods are buried deep in the ground, there is no good example that comes readily to our mind, but shadows of these monasteries can be envisioned at various sites, where later buildings have been located on top of older monuments. This type, too, can be assigned to the Early Historical Period (EHP-1 and EHP-2).

The *Mahavamsa* account of the laying out of the Mahavihara refers to 32 terraces, a pond, a stupa, a building for the Bodhi tree, and several *parivenas*, including a pavilion on the edge of the bathing tank.[24] Despite the wide range of monastic types that has evolved over a period of some 2,000 years, walled terraces containing ritual and domestic structures, linked by steps, pathways, or walled axial avenues yielding long vistas, and pools and water pavilions, are the basic architectural components of such monasteries.

Centric (Metropolitan) Monasteries

The surface remains at Anuradhapura can be assigned to the Late Historical period (LHP), approximately from 600 to 1000 CE. The urban monastic sites confront us however with a continuing colonial legacy.[25] While some ritual monuments are surrounded by empty sand terraces, many are maintained rather like open English parklands with extensive meadows and irregularly scattered trees. Without archaeobotanical evidence it is not possible to identify precisely the original vegetation of these areas. The parklands have been landscaped by archaeologists and the result is largely conditioned by the problem posed by the maintenance of these immense archaeological tracts. The trees present on site have probably not been planted; they are part of the former vegetation and their presence depends on chance. Maintenance, has, however to keep the areas free from spontaneous invasion by the surrounding jungle and extensive pasture land is the most economical way to guarantee this. That is the reason why pasturing cattle is usual in the areas where ruin are found.

The basic plan of the centric monastery, comprising the major monasteries of Anuradhapura, consists of a central stupa surrounded on three or four sides by residential quarters and their related structures. A substantial open area remains between the stupa precinct and the residential area. This large public space was supplied with broad streets giving access to other ritual structures and the sub-monastery complexes – at Anuradhapura these were usually of the *pancayatana* type. Large pools with pavilions at the entrances to the stupas added further interesting elements to the public place from where gated entrances led to private walled avenues. The gates and avenues provided the entrance to individual monasteries of the *pancayatana* type. In the late 19th century, a grove of palms and Bo trees surrounded the sacred Bodhi tree.[26] We can only speculate that public space was sand swept with well-defined tree-lined streets, probably interspersed with densely planted shady groves, very like the ancient public parks already mentioned. The chronicles record that designated mango orchards and gardens of jasmine were planted outside the city wall.

Pancayatana Parivena

These are the most typical grouping of monastic buildings in Anuradhapura. Sub-monasteries possess two types of gardens: the first is the walled precinct in which the *pancayatana*'s five dwelling units are situated with their complement of long walled axial avenues and gatehouses providing formal entry; the second is also a walled compound attached to the *pancayatana* compound but lacking dwelling units or any sacred appurtenances. This space appears today however closer to a secular pleasure garden than anything else. The *pancayatana* plan is highly symmetrical and geometrical. No one has yet explained its appearance, fully formed, sometime in the 6th century, or its enduring appeal to the monastic elders of Anuradhapura.

These monasteries follow a design approach opposite to that seen in the *giri* monasteries. They are highly constructed artificial places where man's authority is stamped on nature. This means that horticulture played a far more significant role in the design of the garden. These gardens connect wealth, power, sophisticated irrigation knowledge and a certain disciplined aesthetic favoured by Buddhist intellectuals of the period.

A *pancayatana* dwelling precinct is entered through an elaborate gatehouse which is connected to it by a walled avenue. The avenue can be very long and subdivided into compartments by smaller gatehouses and open precincts, with short parapet walls. It affords what is clearly intended view of the hierarchical disposition of the two-storey (at minimum) dwelling units in three dimensions and marks a hierarchy of spaces. The avenue precincts are interesting in themselves; they contain rare examples of stone garden furniture – low parapet walls, with austere copings which terminate in pedestals on which are mounted delicately carved urns (*purna ghata*). The avenues give entry into the walled precincts of the *pancayatana*, the latter being rectangular and between 45 x 61 metres and 30 x 37 metres. It is not possible to say precisely how high the precinct walls were originally, but they may have been anything from 1.2 to 2.1 metres.

Courtyard Pool Gardens

This type is not well documented. The pools have been conserved as isolated monuments rather than as elements in a much larger whole. As mentioned, the courtyards of this typology contain the magnificent pools known as the Ath Pokuna and the Kuttam Pokuna, or twin pools. The 3rd-century CE Ath Pokuna is situated in the Maha Nethpa Mula, while the 6th-century Kuttam Pokuna is adjacent to the Kapara Mula; both Mulas were administrative divisions of the Abhayagiri Monastery.

The Ath Pokuna (Elephant Pond): is 159 x 53 metres and 10 metres deep, with tapering sides lined with dressed stones in regular courses *rali pena*. Its enormous size suggests it functioned as a reservoir for at least the western sector of the monastery. Gated entrances with steps lead into the pool on all four sides. The extant 3-metre-high doorframes, on the east and south, indicate that the pool was surrounded by walls (of unknown height) with impressive entrances.

At Anuradhapura the Abhayagiri monastery, with a giant stupa at its centre, was the largest and most striking complex. This aerial view shows the density of constructions and bodies of water; in the middle, the large rectangular Ath Pokuna (Elephant Pond), the not excavated southern pond at the right. The detail gives an impression of the highly geometric arrangements. The whole can be considered today as an immense archaeological park.

The Ath Pokuna was surrounded by monasteries, some with direct access to the water via high door frames.

The splendid excavated and restored Ath Pokuna or Elephant Pond, the largest body of water (53 x 159 m) in the Abhayagiri monastery.

Details of the construction method of the banks and at the southern end the deep sluice well that control the flow of water.

A street bordering the western edge of the pool joined a main street to the north and led to the principal refectory serving the entire community of monks. The pool, though accessible from the street, was hidden or separated from it by a wall. The street also gave access to the high-level western terraces, the water gardens and associated monasteries discussed below. The proximity of the refectory, and a stone-lined channel leading from the Ath Pokuna towards it, suggests that it served the refectory. The water entering the the pool is controlled by a large sluice at the southern end. The pool probably served for bathing and storage.

The Kuttam Pokuna

If the sheer scale and proportions of the vast expanse of water account for the ineffable sensual appeal of the Ath Pokuna, the Kuttam Pokuna (Twin Pond) delights in the repetitive symmetry of its concept, elegant proportions, austere aesthetics and masterful stonework. The pool complex is designated a courtyard because it was most probably surrounded by a wall, albeit now of unknown dimensions (the site was heavily modified during the early days of the modern road construction). The upper surface of the otherwise smooth coping stones of the extant retaining wall of the perimeter pool described below possesses a narrow rough zone along one edge that may perhaps have served as the base for a wall. If this was the case, then we can speculate that an outer wall was present. Access to the perimeter pool was by doors set in this wall. A long east-west axial path with double gateways, recently excavated, appears to connect the pool with the main public thoroughfare leading north from the city, cutting through the main monastery. The pathway aligns with the east-west entrance axis of the pools, implying that theses may have had public access. The relationship of the pools to the adjacent unexcavated and fascinating Kapara Mula monastery is not known.

Another important body of water is the Kuttam Pokuna or Twin Pool, which was part of the Kapara Mula monastery, to the east of the central stupa.

The Kuttam Pokunas are an example of masterful and elegant stonework. Originally the pool complex was in the centre of a courtyard.

The perimeter pool surrounding the twin pools is around 5 metres wide, bounded on the outside by a low stone retaining wall; it is reached by steps leading down from ground level. It was designed to contain water, although water is absent today. The twin pools are laid out on a north-south axis and are accessed via four axial stair entrances in the inner parapet wall of the perimeter pool. The northern pool is 30 metres long and the southern pool 44m, both are 17m wide and 4.2 m deep; their sides are lined with broad, steep, irregular stone steps. The entire ensemble is exquisitely embellished with carved copings, banisters and pedestals with urns. It is guarded by an exceptional five-hooded Naga set into the inner wall around the twin pools.

Abhayagiri Vihara Water Gardens

The so-called golden pool at Abhayagiri is a refined example of a stepped stone pool-courtyard that forms a completely private space. Its austere dressed stonewalls and single-gated entrance give access to a single *pancayatana*. The presence of the gateway confirms the walled arrangement.

The garden in the so-called Sector 1 of the Abhayagiri Vihara, first excavated by Burrows in the 1890s and described further by Bell,[27] has been linked with the Buddhist (Zen) monasteries of Japan (Bandaranayake 1974). The sector contains four monasteries, marked A, B, C and D. A distinguishing feature of the site is the long ridge of boulders running north-south through its centre. The principal entrance to the sector is off a main street running along the western perimeter of the Ath Pokuna mentioned earlier. The site is on much higher ground than the street. The entrance is via steep steps cut through retaining walls that lead up to a gatehouse with an elephant wall. To this complex must be added the monastery on the eastern perimeter of the Ath Pokuna, perched high above it, from where steps descend through a gated entrance into the pool.

Pivotal to the design are the boulder ridge and sloping terrain. The garden is created by subtle

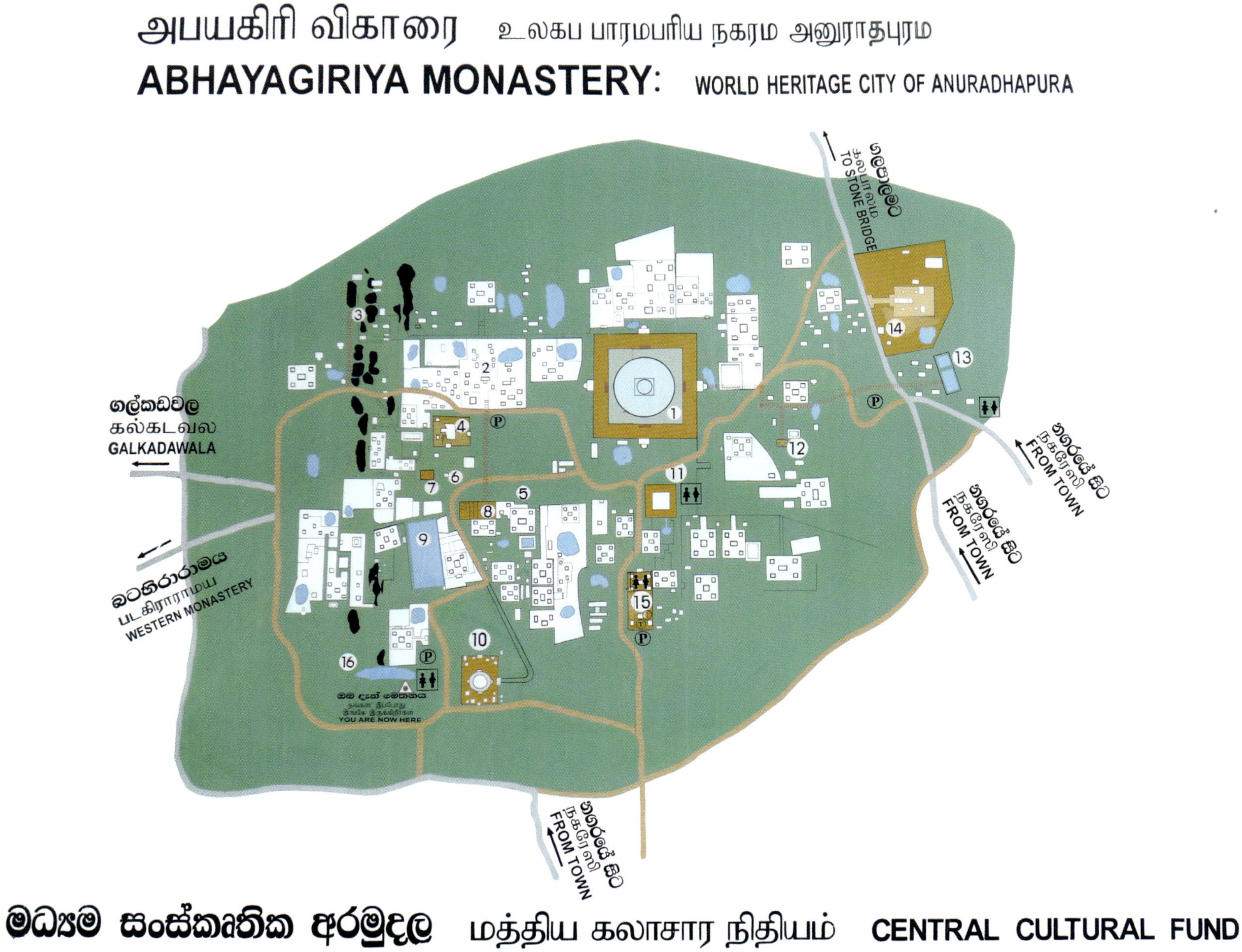

alterations of the topography, to which are added steps, walled precincts, terraces, pavilions on boulders, pools and rock-shelters. Hydraulic engineering skill allowed water to be conveyed to the many pools by means of underground drains connecting the Bulankulam reservoir on the west and the Perimiyam Kulam to the northwest. From the top of the boulder ridge – an outcrop of gneiss 110 metres long, designated rock A – it would have been possible to see the large pools, the Ath Pokuna and the southern pond, and at least seven subsidiary pools serving the complex. Pavilions were constructed on the elongated ridge A to catch the views and the cool breezes rising off large expanses of water. Features associated with *giri* monasteries reappear in the *Gal-ge*. Steps, walls and flat terraces integrate the outcrop of boulders, never more than 8 metres high, into the garden. Existing terraces, grooves for brick walls traversing the sides of the rock and holes for posts cut on the tops of boulders all indicate how the flat terraces made the upper surface of the rock suitable for high-level pavilions. The raised location allowed a 360-degree view of gardens and pools.

The west side of the rock at ground level was scooped out to make a cave which looked out on to its own private walled garden. The cave itself, 4 metres long and 3 metres deep, has a beautifully cut rounded

ABHAYAGIRIYA WATER GARDENS

1 Abhayagiriya Stupa
2 Moonstone
3 Deegha Pasana Cave
4 Ratnaprasada
5 Bodhigara
6 Burrows Pavilion
7 Bodhigara
8 Refectory
9 Elephant Pond
10 Lankarama Complex
11 Assembly Hall
12 Samadhi Buddha Image (sculpture)
13 Twin Ponds
14 Kapara Mula
15 Museum
16 Southern Pond

Photographic reproduction of the official visitors information plan, completed by the author.

roof. It was divided into three compartments and sheltered from the elements by a 60 cm-thick mud wall, protected by a *kotare* drip ledge. Fronting the cave is a narrow, low-slung, undulating boulder into which a *kema* pool 6 x 2.4 metres is cut.[28] We do not know the purpose of the buildings or gardens. The fourth cluster, clearly man-made, is an island of rocks and trees inside an exquisitely proportioned, extended narrow pool: Burrows described it as a beautiful '*pokuna*', prior to excavation in 1891. The asymmetrically placed island inside southern Pokuna (not yet excavated) is perhaps the sole survivor of the water gardens that must once have been a feature of these monasteries.[29]

Some motifs from the so-called sector 1 of the Abhayagiri Vihara Water gardens (sector 1 is situated east of the Ath Pokuna, on the left side of the plan, p. 126).

Top:
The principal entrance to sector 1 is via steep steps through the retaining wall.

Bottom:
The ruins of gatehouses.

Other motifs from the Abhayagiri Water gardens.

Right:
This circular pool is quite exceptional.

Previous pages:

Top left:
The long boulder ridge, rock A. On its western side a cave was cut out, looking out on to its own private garden.

Top right:
A kema pool, part of the garden.

Bottom left:
The unexcavated southern pond with its island.

Bottom right:
An elegant stone-lined pool.

Pabbata (Mountain) Vihara

Of all the ancient monastic types found in Sri Lanka, the *pabbata vihara* is identified as the classic 'Sinhalese' monastery thanks to its position as the precursor of the most typical monastic plan found in Sri Lanka today. These monasteries are poorly excavated and, therefore, the least known and understood. Their garden forms, even less well known, are the most impressive of all, for the reason that their spectacular spatial and tectonic composition includes the gardens.

The ancient term *pabbata*, used to denote this architectural type, is apt since the focus of the design is the construction of a ziggurat of three terraced gardens.[30] In their well-developed form, these monasteries lie on the eastern and northern outskirts of the city of Anuradhapura. They are also to be found at various provincial sites in the south, east and centre including Padikemgala, Vannatipalama and Dimbulagala.[31] From untidy beginnings at Pankuliya, their design evolves into a formal and distinct stereotype where axial planning, symmetry and geometry are primary design tools. While any attempt to date the monasteries is futile, it is known that the surface remains belong between the 8th and 10th centuries.[32] The best examples of these highly schematic arrangements are Pacinatissapabbata, Puliyankulam and Toluvila, at Anuradhapura. They were royal monasteries endowed and built by the monarch of Anuradhapura. For the most part, the designs make little concession to nature, in fact the opposite. At the same time, boulders on site and water courses are incorporated into the design.

The *pabbata viharas* were closely connected with the central monasteries of the Abhayagiri Vihara, whose occupants were sympathetic to Mahayanist thought. The obviously pre-planned formal architectural layout is attributed to Mahayana practice.[33]

Even in their present state of woeful neglect, the power of the brilliantly innovative spatial concept of the formal design cannot fail to impress the visitor. The only way to grasp it is to visualise the space in its entirety as a ziggurat, or sequence of three receding quadrangular terrace gardens surrounded by a high boundary wall and a moat, with one or several entrance gateways with commanding views. The construction of stepped terrace-gardens was a considerable feat of civil and hydraulic engineering and management. It

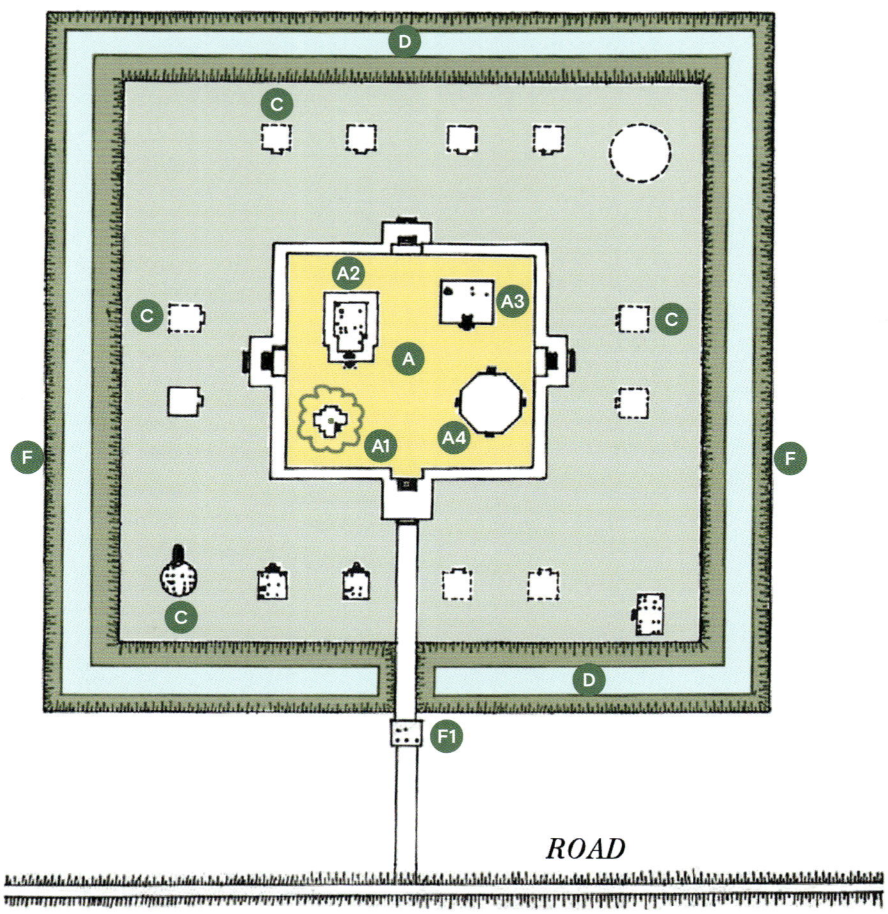

PACINATISSAPABBATA

A Sacred precinct
A1 Bodhigara, Bodhi-tree Shrine
A2 Patimaghara, Image house
A3 Uposathagara, major monastic residence
A4 Stupa
C Residential buildings
D Moat
F Outer precinct
F1 Main Entrance

Source: Sen. Bandaranayake, *Sinhalese Monastic Architecture*, 1975, plan adapted by the author.

required formidable human labour resources and a range of expert knowledge for clearing, excavating, quarrying, building drains, pools and terraces with stairs, bridges, pathways and ritual structures and, finally, for planting.

Nothing is known of the horticulture essential to complete the spatial concept. It may be that the upper terrace resembled the sand-swept gardens of Dambadeniya in the northwest or Yatagala near Galle in the south, later versions of the *Pabbata Vihara*. Pools in the water garden may have attracted birds and been full of lotus, lily and fish. Boating and swimming may have been subsidiary activities. The largest of the gardens is the residential terrace. Whichever way one looked from here, the entire spatial layout of walls, streets, pools and elevated ritual gardens with their magnificent architecture would have been visible. Flowering trees would have added shade and scent. The massive investment of resources and the primary focus on ritual structures indicate that the monasteries served the community at large. Despite the austere nature of the extant architectural ruins, the original inhabitants unquestionably enjoyed a secure luxurious environment.

The Alahana Parivena at Polonnaruwa

The stereotype plan of the *Pabbata Vihara* continued into the Polonnaruwa period and, although not well studied, the Dalada Maluwa, or sacred quadrangle, and the Alahana Parivena display the basic principles of this type. The latter is the largest monastery at Polonnaruwa; built on a gigantic scale, it lacks the geometric precision of its predecessors. The formal pool-terrace garden is absent at Polonnaruwa. The plan of the ritual terraced garden of the classic *Pabbata Vihara* is discernible in the Kandy period monasteries, but without the *uposathagara*. The water gardens and residential terrace gardens disappeared.

The earliest reference to a ruler residing at Polonnaruwa in the *Culavamsa*, is to Aggabodhi IV, 626-641 CE.[34] One has to remember that Polonnaruwa functioned as an alternate royal residence, if not temporary capital, from the reign of Aggabodhi IV, long before the time of the *Culavamsa's* hero Parakramabahu I.

The Alahana Parivena stands on an extensive oblong plateau to the north of the citadel, with the site consisting of four rising terraces linked by flights of steps. The retaining walls were made of rubble and moulded brick, and *makara* (dragon) spouts drained water off the higher terraces. The entire compound was surrounded by an outer brick wall of 573 x 295 metres, and the main entrance was on the east side.

The two lower terraces were allocated for dwelling units regularly arranged as a series of separate courts, each forming a self-contained unit with the required additional buildings. There were several pools serving the dwellings, possibly on their own, but with interconnected walled courtyards[35] – an arrangement closer to the dwelling courtyards of the urban monasteries of Anuradhapura. Here, the upper two terraces contain ritual buildings. The colossal multi-storeyed (around 12) Baddhasimapasada served a mixed residential and ecclesiastical function, occupying the uppermost terrace. No other monastery accorded such a degree of importance to this building type.[36]

The second terrace is dominated by an image-house without precedent – the Lankatilaka – with its massive doorways, fluted columns and a statue of the Buddha over 17 metres tall. The original shrine would have been around 27 metres high.[37] Beside it is a smaller stupa, the Kiri Vihara. The three edifices dominate the entire complex. In terms of garden design, this monastery marks a significant break with earlier *pabbata vihara*. Here the subtle interplay of sheets of water acting as reflecting pools for the ziggurat is lost. Although the terraces remain, the grand spatial conception competes with lofty buildings. 'Ponds and sheets of water reflected the forms of the main buildings and the flowering trees which were planted at intervals must have contributed to the serenity of the scene. Natural boulders were made to harmonise with the scheme of building and the various buildings no doubt sat easily in their surroundings.'[38]

The tradition of incorporating ponds and streams running across the site is also visible at the earlier Kaludiya Pokuna near Sigiriya, and at Yatagala near Galle, where the shifting garden terraces and ponds, recall design principles of the ancient Pabbata vihara.

Today the Gal Vihara monastery, north from the Alahana Parivena, with its statues of extraordinary beauty is praised as a haven of calm amidst an open park, the latter in the past possibly filled with fruit trees and flowering plants. The solitary pond added to the elegance of the garden scene.[39] The image-house in its original context probably belonged to a monastery and was set in a walled compound. There is no evidence that isolated ritual buildings stood in parks. The cherished contemporary parkscape may owe more to British colonial fantasy than anything else.

Padhanagara Parivena (Meditation Monasteries)

While this monastic type has aroused much lively debate,[40] there is agreement, however, that the major activity conducted in them was meditation. The type is also tentatively linked with asceticism and cave dwelling. Several architectural features distinguish this type from the monasteries encountered so far, among them the low priority assigned to ritual buildings, a secluded wilderness location, extreme severity of architecture, the presence of circular structures and superbly carved ornamental urinal stones. Due to the insignificance of ritual structures, a public role is not ascribed to this type. The relationship of the units with rural or semi-urban communities, on whom they must surely have relied for material sustenance, and their location, vis-a-vis the larger urban landscape, remains unexplored.

The origins of the monasteries are dated anywhere between the 5th and 7th centuries. The best documented are the so-called fourteen *Western Monasteries* at Anuradhapura, located in the wilderness, west of the Abhayagiri Vihara. The monastic type is also found near the city of Mihintale, Mullegala and at several provincial sites such as Viharabandigala, Ritigala, Manakanda and Arankale, albeit poorly excavated. However, they are not unique to Sri Lanka. A somewhat similar 8th-century CE complex, with explicit connections to Sri Lanka, survives at the Ratu Baka plateau in central Java, Indonesia, on a hilltop south of the famous contemporary Prambanan Hindu temple complex.[41] The Sailendra inscription 792 CE, of the Javanese regent, commemorates the founding of a branch of the Abhayagiri Vihara of Sinhalese ascetics, 'trained in the sayings of discipline of the Best of the Jinas'.[42]

The double-platform terrace, contained within the inner walled compound, approached through substantial storied gateways, has baffled scholars. In contrast to other monastic types, here residence and ritual combine on the upper or double-platform terrace. In its entirety this monastic type consists of one or several enclosed double-platform terrace units, sometimes as many as fifty, as found at Ritigala, serviced by various ancillary buildings and pools. In general, the sites present an irregular array of buildings and pools connected by stone-lined and sometimes paved pathways, some straight and others curving sinuously. Due to insufficient data, it cannot be said with certainty that the sites were enclosed by outer boundary walls, although Kaludiya Pokuna in Mihintale suggests this was the case.

The only clearly identified structures in these monasteries are the refectory, *jantaghara* and lavatory complex with highly ornate urinals, situated just outside the main enclosure wall. An open urinal, regularly placed north of the upper terrace is a prominent feature of the walled garden. Whether it was enclosed is difficult to say but the Kaludiya Pokuna has a small brick surround. Whether the ornate urinal had a ritual function is disputed.

The monasteries are invariably sited on clusters of boulders, both on level ground and on hills, with access to rock-shelters. Large pools and lakes were fed from channels connected with the greater reservoir systems of Anuradhapura or those especially constructed for the purpose such as at Arankale or Mihintale. Ritigala and Arankale are located on mountain slopes where community structures occurred below, and residential units are found scattered randomly at higher levels. The main structure comprises a rectangular basal terrace leading on to a middle terrace on which sit the double platforms. The floor level of the double platform forms the upper terrace. The two lower terraces are surrounded by stone and brick (or mud) walls whose estimated height is over 2.4 metres.[43] The middle terrace was approached by three axial doorways on the east, north and south. The outer boundary walls of the lower terraces are not extant, but their stone foundations, and sometimes elaborate stone porches, confirm their existence. The outer terraces, at times level with the middle terrace, are around 3–4 metres in width. They are occasionally raised well above ground level on rubble revetments.

The Sri Lankan upper terrace (double platform) is usually built on an east-west axis. The upper terrace is around 0.9 metres high and split by a gangway. Steps on either side of the gangway (sometimes roofed) lead down to the rectangular middle terrace. The rear section of the terrace is a rectangle, approximately 12.2 x 9 metres, usually built onto a boulder, frequently surrounded by a pool and always surmounted by a tile-roof dwelling pavilion. The larger front portion of the terrace is roughly 15.2 x 11.5 metres. It has no roof and its purpose is unknown.[44] On occasion, minor structures of unknown function were also found on this terrace. As a rule, the architectural components are austere, but the presence of a raised cornice and *punkalasas* at the top of stair balustrades to the front platform is recorded.[45] The slabs that form the gangway of the upper terrace are among the 'most ambitious single components employed by the Sinhalese stone mason'.[46] The quality of the stone work is exceptional, and the construction of the monasteries must have incurred heavy financial outlay, a coast as yet not computed.

Not much attention has been paid to the greatly tailored flat middle terrace with its boulders, pools, steps and often a wide elevated platform, the *cankamana*, running on the inside of the boundary wall. But we would not be far wrong in describing this terrace as a

Aerial views over the Alahana Parivena at Polonnaruwa. It is easy to distinguish the different terraces on different levels. In the middle is the upper terrace with the stupa and the Lankatilaka image-house. Many pools of different sizes form part of the gardens.

'secret courtyard garden'. The size of the garden varies, but the largest is in the range of 30 x 44 metres and is thus a little smaller than the walled gardens of the *pancayatana parivena*. The garden, as noted, was in fact surrounded by another terrace with access porches and, presumably, equally high walls. Pillar stumps supported canopies for statues in monasteries H, I and J. A urinal with a lion motif, without a walled brick enclosure, was placed adjacent to the canopy in I. Stone couches for reclining in the entrance porches are frequently mentioned. Situated adjacent to the lake, stone couches and double platforms with urinals can also be seen at Kaludiya Pokuna, Mihintale.

Scholars have remarked on the invasive formal architecture of this monastic type whose scale and materials were alien to the forest.[47] Yet, the powerful visual impression the edifice would have made on anyone who encountered one in the wilderness has been largely ignored. The structures announced their presence through a daunting, austere display of relatively high walls and storied gateways (2.4–4.5m).[48] High walls occurring in the context have been mentioned already (the wall heights of the *pabbata viharas* are not known). Similarly, we are ignorant as to their colour and any paintings that might have decorated them.

The Meditation Monasteries have, annexed to the refectory, a small lavatory complex with often highly ornate urinals. Whether the latter had a ritual function is disputed.

A Secret Garden

The double platform secret garden proper is a walled enclosure comprising the manicured middle terrace, built on to a large boulder. The undulating contours of the boulder interrupt the otherwise level floor of the terrace, contributing to the unique aesthetic sense of the garden. At times, the boulder was cut to form a precise rectangular pool surrounding the rear part of the upper terrace. Often, the boulder was further moulded to create another pool with natural contours. The small roofed pavilion perched on the rear portion was spatially balanced by the large empty terrace facing it; it was the only item of any height inside the garden. The gardens differ from conventional ritual sites in the invariable presence of water. It is difficult to say what plants were included in this boulder, sand and water garden. The surrounding space might have also contributed shade, colour and movement.

Water introduced a combination of movement and stillness into sacred spaces. It seems likely that some shade trees were planted. However, the pools' utilitarian functions may have been secondary to other ritual and aesthetic roles they performed. Due to the constricted format, they may not have contained the usual fish, flowers and birds. Water was always associated with the consecration rites of kings and the initiation ceremonies of monks.[49] The aesthetic and spatial configuration of the secret garden is unique. The designs display a taste for the elemental qualities of rocks, water and sand, which, for the first time in monastic designs, consistently appear together in a confined space. Geometric precision is the hallmark of the walls, terraces, and the boulder pool around the building. These are accompanied by other, equally highly constructed boulder pools and floors which appear totally natural. The forest location merely compounds the mystery surrounding the designs. Their contrived simplicity belies their utter strangeness and the complex mental world of the master designers who conceived them. They must have belonged to a highly skilled, exclusive literate group, fluent in the mysteries of handling ritual space, design artifice and construction techniques. The silent ruins encountered today hardly allow us to grasp the extraordinary quality of the design. This is not just because the walls, roofs, water, sand, plants and colour have all disappeared, but also because their sophisticated forms spoke to a discerning and cultured community whose spiritual-aesthetic language and cultural repertoire are profoundly unfamiliar to us.

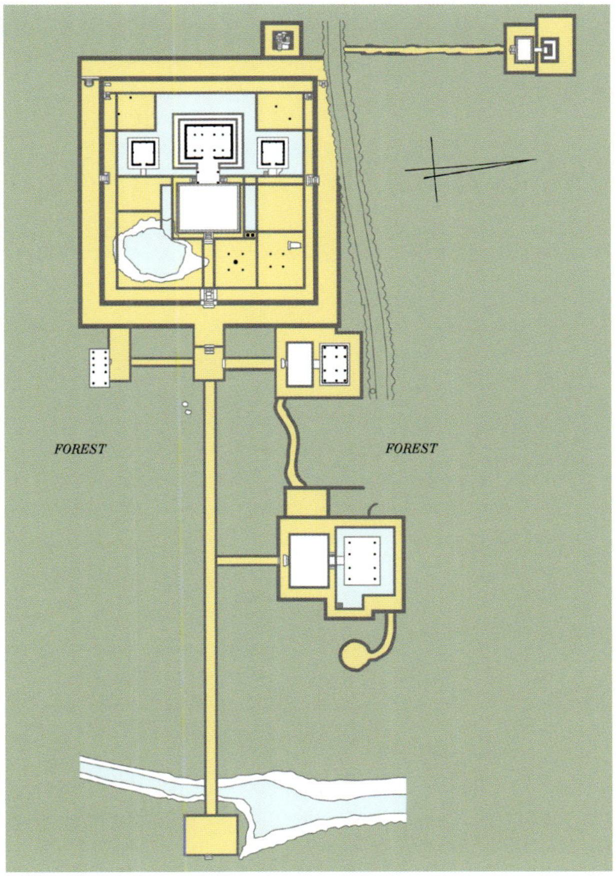

A typical plan of one of the fourteen Western Monasteries: monastery I. All present a highly geometric and austere design and masterful stonework.

The monasteries possessed another type of open water garden whose central feature was a large pool or lake, the best example of which is the Kaludiya Pokuna where the double platform unit and other dwelling types are closely integrated with the lake. One of the most skilful aspects of this design lies in the exploitation of the reflective potential of the deep water to bring distant mountain ranges into the immediate experience of the garden. The shifting stillness, movement and colour of the water are always a part of the sensual experience. Moreover, intriguing outlines of dry lakebeds and pools are still visible at the Western monastery sites.

The secret gardens at Abhayagiri, Kaludiya Pokuna and Ritigala, linked by independent sources to royal patronage, *Pamsukulin* ascetics and Vajrayana practitioners, raise the possibility that their unique spatial formation was related to esoteric Buddhist practices, but what exactly these were is unknown. Scholars have yet to explain why secrecy and sophistication combine in the wilderness. Why did these monasteries exert an irresistible pull on kings and wealthy patrons? Although a public role is not assigned to them, it is unlikely that the private spiritual endeavours of a few monks tucked away in the forest invited such lavish patronage. How do we reconcile appurtenances such as small ritual items, urinals and stone couches with ascetic practice? Whether the term 'ascetic' is appropriate to cover the ambiguities and unknown lives lived in these monasteries remains an open question.

To close this section, we propose to illustrate the extraordinary landscape architecture of monastic gardens with three examples: Kaludiya Pokuna at Mihintale, Ritigala and Arankäle.

Details of Western Monasteries.

Top left:
An example of an enclosure wall with the entrance gate.

Top right:
Example of how trees might have been integrated into the enclosed space.

Bottom left:
Example of a gatehouse with benches on both sides (monastery I). View of double platforms surrounded by moats (monastery I).

Bottom right:
Lotus pool showing how natural rocks are integrated into the manmade architecture (monastery I).

Kaludiya Pokuna

Kaludiya Pokuna monastery nestles in a small valley at the foothills between the towering *Aeth Vehera kanda* and the *Anaikutikanda,* the southernmost peak of the ranges forming the Mihintale hills. During the late Anuradhapura period, these sites of ancient occupation came to be associated with Mahayana Buddhism. The Mihintale Trikaya inscription of the 7th century and the Indikatuseya monastery' copper plaques from the 8th or 9th centuries CE are in Sanskrit and deal with Mahayana beliefs and texts.[50]

The Kaludiya Pokuna ruins can broadly be assigned to this period. They are dominated by an exquisite small lake which is part man-made and part natural, whose contours comprise dressed stone embankments that weave around boulders rising from the waters. The ruins can be divided into five groups purely for ease of understanding: an entrance pathway of narrow stone steps that curves sinuously through boulders and trees on the north west; a set of geometrically laid out ritual terraces with a stupa and perhaps another ritual structure to the north; a line of geometrical avenues that border the lake on the west, affording entrance to the elevated stone and brick walled terraces of a *padhanagara parivena*, with a well-defined *cankamana* below it; pavilions built on boulders and cave shelters linked both to the lake and to the southern hill.

In the centre of the south-western lake shore a high natural rock (perhaps a meditation rock), with carved and polished seats at its top, accessible by stone steps, is the spatial and spiritual heart, the focus of the whole. The meditation seats were probably once protected by a pavilion. On the eastern side of the lake three existing boulders afforded the opportunity to build an island in a surprising ship's form, crowned by a platform with a pavilion. Even if the pavilion has disappeared, the theme of the island pavilion is very present, like the water pavilions at Sigiriya and Anuradhapura. While the secret garden is still present in the walled enclosure of the double-platform terrace, here one can clearly recognize its relationship to the larger water garden with pavilions, hinted at in Bell's description above. There is evidence that the terraces were surrounded by one or two sets of boundary walls.[51]

The fragmentary nature of the northern ritual terrace defies further analysis, it could be a later addition. Nevertheless, De Silva[52] implies that its location, distant from the residential terrace, allowed the public to perform their devotions without disturbing the monks. Whether the public had access to this monastic type as originally conceived is unclear. The entrance stairway to the monastery immediately transports one into the environment of a boulder garden where the asymmetry of nature is paramount. The steps wind through an array of shapely boulders and shady trees while the sound of birds accompanies the gentle climb. On reaching the monastic level proper, after entry through a constricted gatehouse, the surprise is consummate. The eye confronts the incessant movement and changing colours

The Kaludiya Pokuna monastery and its lake are situated between the foot of the high Ath Vihara kanda mountain to the east, with the ruins of a stupa on its summit, and the Anaikutikanda to the south, a boulder hill with caves for hermits, in a natural hollow.

KALUDIYA POKUNA

1 Entrance gate
2 Ruin of a stupa
3 Residential buildings
4 Double terrace
5 Meditation rock
6 Island in ship's form, pavilion
7 Access to the lake for ritual bathing
8 Anaikutti kanda, inhabited hermit caves
9 Rajagirilen kanda, ancient Giri monastery
10 Ät Vihara kanda, ruin of a stupa

Drawing: Klaus Holzhausen, based on measurements on the site by the author.

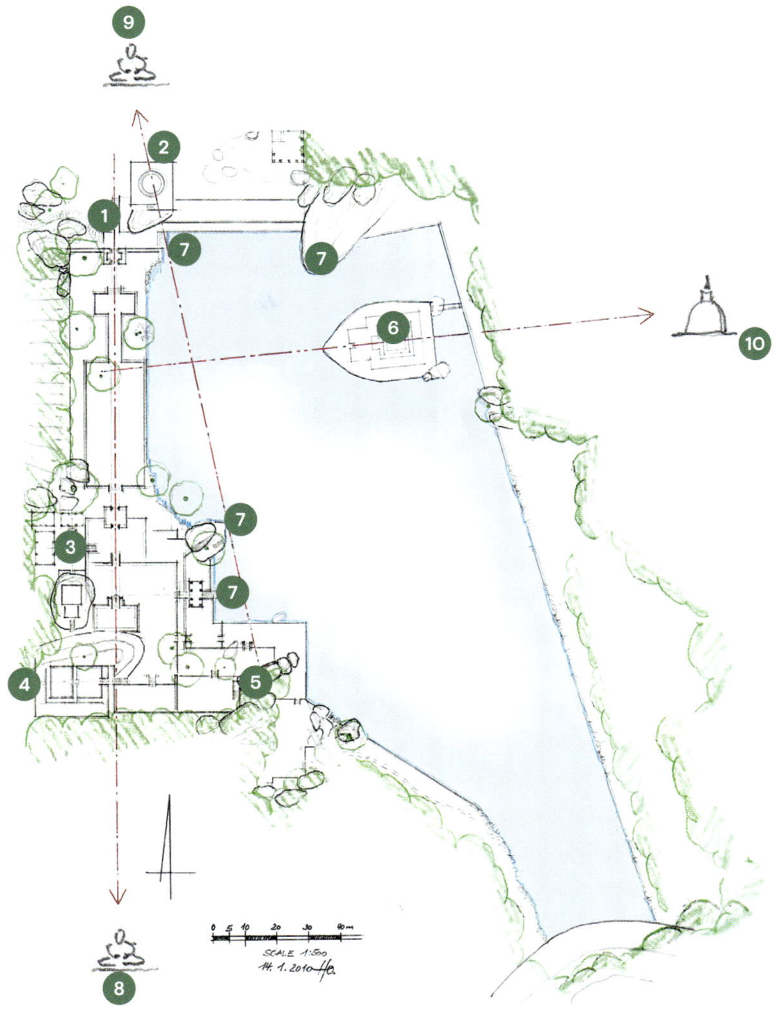

of shadows and reflections on the surface of a large, beautiful boulder lake. The lake is the cynosure of the garden. At this level, apart from the lake and boulders, everything else is highly contrived and designed so that the geometry of the planning enhances the natural landscape. The asymmetry of the lake contrasts with the straight lines.

As usual, the dressed stonework is immaculate and the architecture austere. The entrance gateway is a stone structure that was probably storied and tied into high brick walls that have disappeared. It leads onto a southern series of formal rectangular terraced avenues that keep rising until they reach the main double platform ritual cum dwelling terrace situated at the highest point of the site. This is built onto a large boulder with the aid of dressed stone retaining walls pierced at regular intervals by finely cut stone steps. The avenues also give entry to a cluster of cave shelters on the west, set into another large boulder. They are provided with stone roofs, walls and windows and open onto a small terrace of their own. The summit of the same boulder, reached via steps linking three flat terraces, supported a small pavilion. At the base of the boulder is a pool cut into it. On the east, bordering the lake, the avenue gave access to a different type of structure which appears to have been a kind of bath house with bridge terraces leading to a flight of steps giving access to the water. Adjacent to this, overlooking the water and on a special terrace, is a beautifully carved stone seat with a curved back for reclining which continues behind the boulders to another stone cut seat with moulded back.

In Kaludiya Pokuna one particularity is striking: the visual relations with the landscape that surrounds it that recall the Japanese principle of 'shakkei' (the borrowed landscape). The monastery was created in the focal point of the elements of the surrounding landscape, with the lake as the central element. In addition, visual axes create clear relationships with the three surrounding mountains: from the entrance portico, the axis of the main avenue is directed exactly at the top of Anaikuttikanda, a set of boulders that house numerous cave dwellings,

some of which are still inhabited today by hermit monks; from the meditation rock in the centre, an axis passes by the old stupa in the north of the lake and aims at the top of Rajagirilenkanda, an ancient *giri* monastery. From a point on the main avenue an axis connects the tip of the boat island with the top of Aeth Vehera, the dominant mountain, which was crowned by a large white stupa, now in ruins. The pyramidal mountain is symmetrically reflected in the lake. Taking into account the visual impact and logic of this network of links, one may ponder whether the ideas of the monks did not go even further – to project a relationship between these horizontal visual links and the cosmos.

Just as at Sigiriya, there is provision for a multitude of pavilions and garden seats to enjoy cool breezes and lake views. As at Abhayagiriya, the island pavilion reproduces the leisure provisions for monarchs, implying that such a garden architecture was not, in fact, solely the prerogative of kings. Once more, a refined corporeal and intellectual theme of pleasure guided the designs of gardens which purportedly served a handful of meditating monks.

In the chapter 'Sacred landscapes from Delphi to Yosemite' of his book *A World of Gardens* John Dixon Hunt mentions the phenomenon of surprise experienced by a stroller in approaching the sanctuary of Apollo at Delphi: its gradual appearance and disappearance, then its entire and sudden revelation. The famous garden historian qualifies the site as 'sublime' and 'sacred'. The monastery of Kaludiya Pokuna impresses the visitor in a similar way: from the road one has no idea where the paved walk that climbs through trees and rocks will leave, at least until arriving on the summit. There two stone porticoes appear surrounded by ruined masses of brick and typical frangipani trees which suggest something beyond. Upon approaching, one of the porticoes at the left reveals a lake, while the other, to the right, frames a landscape with an axis from which a succession of small pavilions fan out. Here, similarly to Sigiriya, the aesthetic topic is the contrast between the axial geometry and the organic character of rocks.

The entrance stairway leads through a kind of natural boulder garden. Climbing the steps, one cannot see the destination until the last moment, when, on arriving at the monastery level, a small gatehouse appears set between the ruins of the former enclosure wall.

After entering through the gatehouse, the surprise is perfect: the vista in all its beauty opens out. Looking back, to the right of the gate, above a high retaining wall, the ruins of a stupa are visible.

A straight avenue through rectangular terraces leads to the rock summit of the Anaikutikanda. This is one of the monastery's visual axes.

Hermit monks from a small community, living in the Anaikutikanda caves, come to the lake shore to wash and to bathe.

Top:
An unusual rock formation, a kind of promontory in the middle of the western lakeside, was probably used as a meditation rock, as a stairway was constructed with steps cut into the rock that give access to the summit. From the top of the rock, a visual relation with the ancient Rajagirilenkanda Giri monastery is evident.

Bottom:
The ship-like island, the meditation rock and the double platform terrace are clearly visible even in this photograph, taken when the water level was rather low.

Top:
The highest boulder is terraced by walls,; the steps lead to the upper double platform terrace.

Bottom:
The second terrace to the left is surrounded by a moat and linked to the first terrace by a stone bridge.

Overlooking the water, on a terrace, is a beautifully carved stone seat.

A large boulder crowned by a terrace, on which once stood a wooden pavilion. Access steps are to the left.

A group of monks' dwellings at the west side of the avenue, on a lower level. Under the boulder in front, a cave shelter with a stone façade.

Two examples of a borrowed landscape, what the Japanese call 'Shakkei'.

Left:
Even from a distance of 1 km, the Rajagirilenkanda boulder mountain forms a part of the lake landscape.

Right:
The high Ath Vehara kanda is so imposing that its pyramid is reflected in the lake. Both mountains are also in the line of sight, the first from the meditation rock, the second from the main avenue.

Ritigala Kanda

The main peak of the mountain range is identified as Ritigala Kanda with monastery at the site classed as a *padhanagara parivena* and is situated on the southern slope of a hill some 766 metres high. The massif rises abruptly, dominating the surroundings plains of the North Central Province, and its forest cover remains green throughout the year while mist and cloud envelop the summit during the monsoons. It is isolated from other mountain ranges. Numerous boulders crossed by many streams are the main feature of the site. Here, of course, there is no open water garden as found on the plains. However, there are more than 70 known cave dwellings associated with the range, varying in size from one- to five-room clusters; the monks shared central facilities.

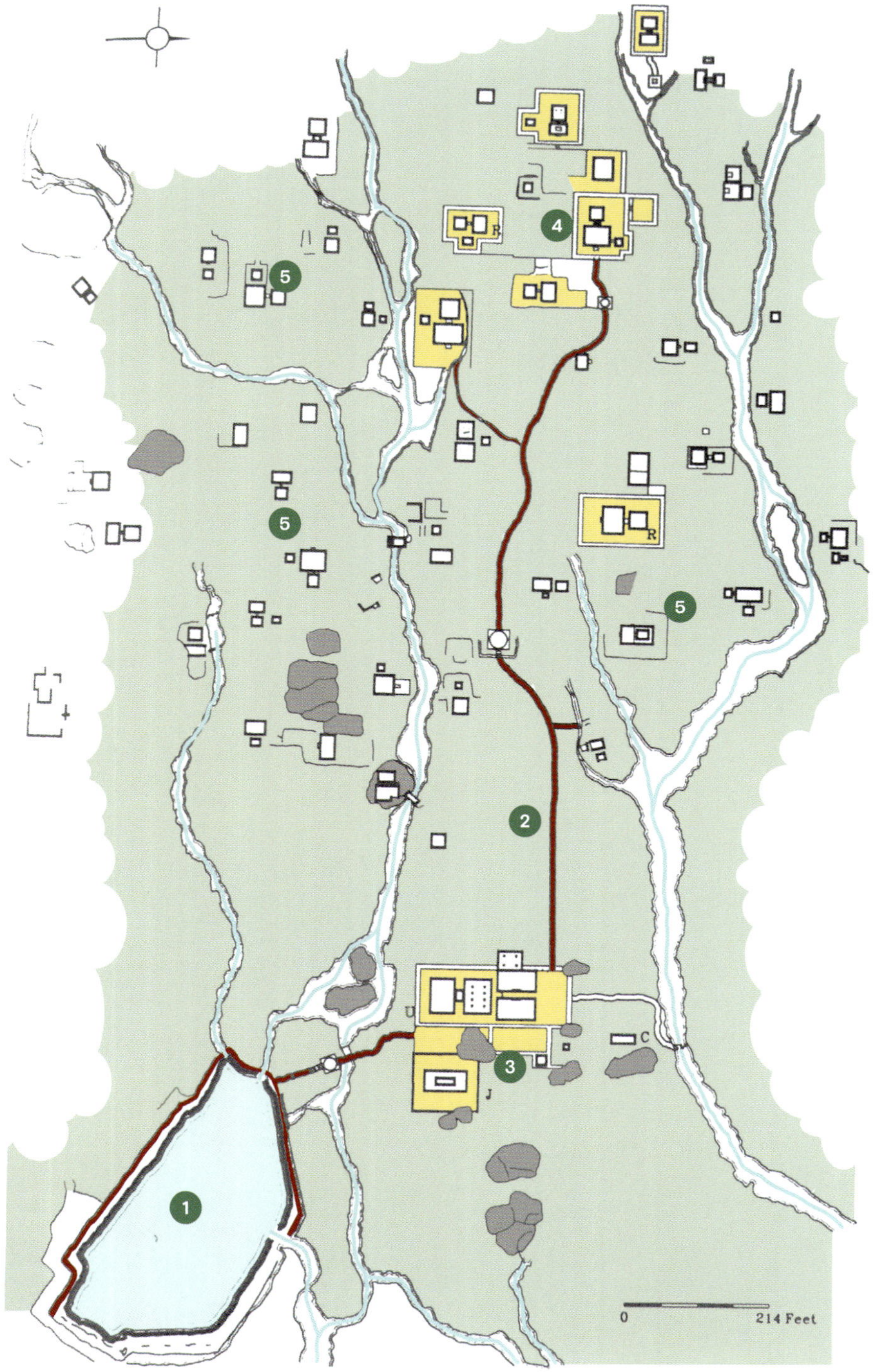

RITIGALA

1 Central Pond, Reservoir
2 Main Pathway
3 Monastic Buildings
4 Monastic Buildings
5 Residential Buildings

Source: Senake Bandaranayake, *Sinhalese Monastic Architecture*, 1975, adapted by the author.

The Ritigala monastery is spread over a large hillside in the forest. The main design element is the long walkway, adapted to the terrain, which maintains throughout the same width of 1,80 m and the same perfect stonework, comprising of stairs and small squares of varying design. The walkway connects the monks' dwellings with the ritual buildings and the communal facilities.

An example showing how the builders overcame the difficulties of the rather chaotic natural boulder and forest terrain.

Top:
Ruin of a building with a courtyard.

Bottom:
A double-platform building with, to the right, a cancamana, a sand path for walking meditation.

More views of the pathways through the forest.

The main design consists of a central pathway 1.8m wide and about 530 metres long that links the communal facilities and the monks' dwellings to a large enclosed compound on higher ground. The compound is similar to those at Anuradhapura monasteries and was possibly the residence of the chief monk. The pathway is lined with neatly dressed stone slabs and stone kerbs demarcate its limits. The path follows the natural topography, traverses the forest, constantly climbing and winding upwards, at times with resting places, steps and bridges crossing streams. More than 50 double-platform terraced gardens lead off the main path; they were not surrounded by enclosure walls. Further sinuous man-made paths link the whole. These monasteries enjoyed the secluded wild beauty of the forest. A small but deep lake supplied water to the entire complex.

The embankment of the central water reservoir at ground level; the reservoir was probably also used for bathing. The pond had only recently been cleaned up from the jungle that covered it. The perfectly restored stonework is impressive.

Arankäle

The ancient entrance to the monastery of Arankäle (early Anuradhapura period, 8th-10th century BCE) is located in the countryside north of the town of Kurunegala, at the foot of a forest-covered hill. After passing a very popular temple, the visitor arrives in front of a first group of boulders with cave dwellings and an image house. It is today the starting point for the visit to the old monastery complex. The ancient entrance was at the opposite end, near the hot water bath. One has to skirt the boulders, which still hide it, to reach the start of an extraordinary itinerary. What a bold move to build this path straight through forests and clearings for about 600 metres!

The straight line connects the monks' dwellings and the communal buildings and creates a strong contrast with the surrounding irregular and organic nature. The unevenness is contrasted and punctuated by a series of stone stairs. All these segments of the path are horizontal and covered with sand, bordered on both sides by perfectly cut stone slabs. They pass over the irregularities of the ground, crossing hollows held by small walls. The path, whose width does not vary – it always measures 1,80 metres, or 2,60 metres including the borders – passes through three small squares, one of them circular while the others rectangular in shape, which serve as a connection to the lateral paths leading to the ancient dwellings located higher up, which form terraces in the forest, each of which equipped with one of the mysterious double platforms. One of them in the south-western area, the best preserved and excavated, is a stonework of incredible craftmanship and beauty.

The linear path is not a visual axis; one cannot see the end of it, it is discovered step by step because of the forest and the approximately 9-10 metres difference in level between its beginning and its end. It is only from the Bodhigara clearing that one can see the large pool and the communal buildings through the trees. At the end of the 600 metre path one arrives at a rectangular site which allows a change of direction of 90° to the right and, after another 65 metres, leads towards a complex of constructions, of which only the basic walls and the bases of the

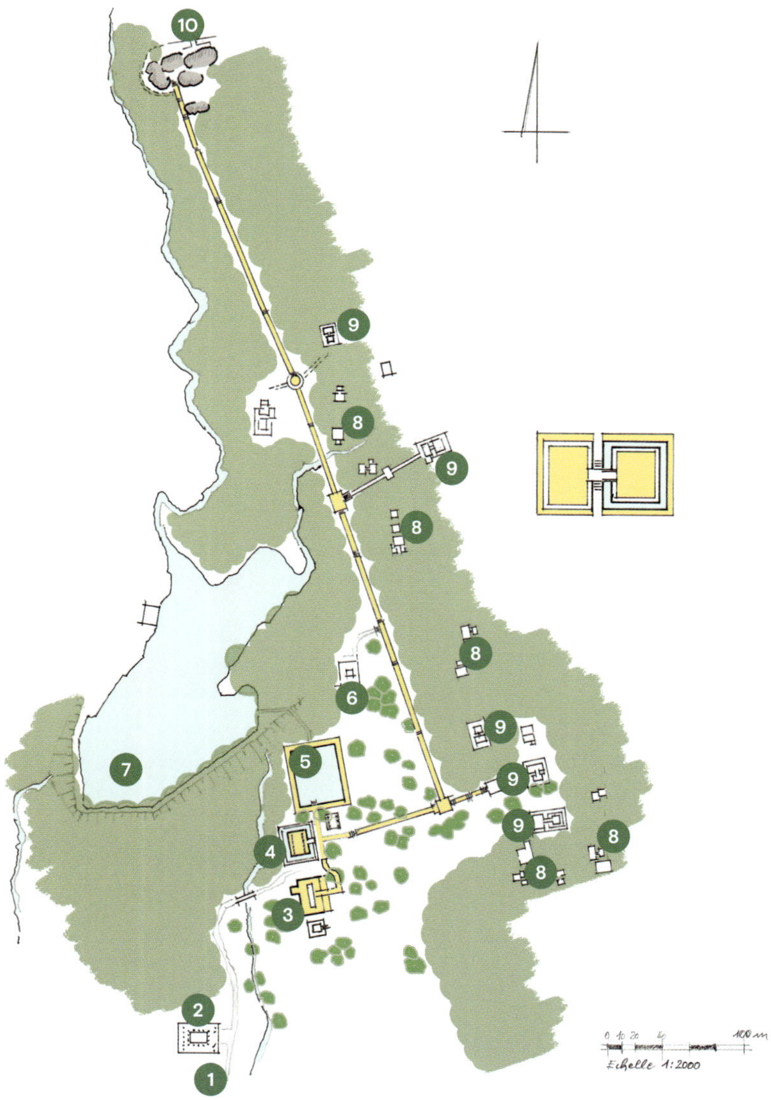

ARANKÄLE

1 Ancient entrance
2 Bathhouse, hot water bath
3 Refectory
4 Chapter house
5 Rectangular pond
6 Bodhi Tree shrine
7 Water reservoir lake, today abandoned
8 Residential buildings
9 Double platforms
10 Image house, cave

Drawing: Klaus Holzhausen
Sources: on site measurements by the author
Nimal De Silva, *Landscape Tradition of Sri Lanka*, 1996, adapted by the author

Top:
This image-house cave is the starting point for a visit to the Arankäle archaeological site.

Bottom:
A long central pathway is the most surprising design element. After descending some steps, the sand path goes straight through the forest and over the uneven terrain for about 600 m, crossing two squares, one rectangular the other circular, connecting the monks' dwellings above in the forest. Its width, 2.60 m including the stone borders, never varies.

Bottom left:
This rectangular square marks the turn of 90° and connects the staircase leading to a cluster of monks' dwellings and double platforms in the forest above.

Top right:
one of the double platforms.

Bottom right:
Near the refectory and the convention hall, in the centre of the monastery, is a beautiful stone-lined rectangular pool measuring 33 x 42 m.

columns are preserved. It was a refectory and a chapter house surrounded by a moat. This group of buildings, probably multi-storied, was the centre of the monastery. A surprising exception to the strict geometry is the winding, organic path that connects the buildings. This complex is bounded on the east by a large rectangular pool of about 42 x 33 metres, framed by stepped stones and full of lotus and water lilies. A little further east, an abandoned reservoir lake, whose waters are fed by a river and kept in place by a dam now covered by overgrown greenery, served as water supply for the entire monastery.

The austere architecture and the strict and rational geometry of the built elements were integrated into the existing surroundings in a discreet way. Everything was built with consideration to the natural topography, its terraces, waterways, boulders and the existing vegetation. From the point of view of the landscape architect, Arankäle is a very powerful example of a monastic garden, even if the landscape setting is not extraordinary. It is the design itself that is of exceptional quality and shows the length to which Buddhist monks could go in terms of intellectual and spiritual exuberance.

Conclusion

The above sites present monastic landscapes that reflect the values of celibate asceticism associated with the wilderness, the *nec plus ultra* of social conduct.[53] It is very probable that Buddhist ascetics of different orders opted for many different lifestyles and meditation techniques. Thus, the ascetic ideal may have occupied a moral highground and an exalted place in the mental world of the designers who imagined monastic landscapes, and the aristocrats and householders who endowed them. We cannot say with certainty whether the restrained aesthetics, thematised in the design traditions encountered here, embodied the ideal of renunciation. But there exists a distinct possibility that a taste for a particular abstract aesthetic – otherwise described 'as a kind of architectural tidiness of mind'[54] or a signal reference to the profound concept of 'cessation' – held special appeal for designers of monastic gardens.

The gardens of the great urban and provincial monasteries are long lost to us. Many of the *giri* monasteries still in use have been altered over time. Yet, hidden in them are traces of older garden design uses, traditions that seem to have the ability to evoke a sense of mystery and suspense by almost freezing time, as it were. The physical features of the site are suffused with a depth of time that escapes modern designs. Through the assembly of scattered evidence, we can gain a faint understanding of what the gardens were like and the part they may have played in the life of the people. It may be futile to search for what these places meant to those who commissioned, designed and used them, because their mental universes were very different from our own.

Top left:
The convention hall platform, surrounded by a moat, is accessible via a bridge.

Top right:
The refectory and chapter house are connected by a stone-lined sand pathway, its rare, curved organic form contrasting with the overall geometric design.

Next page:
The ruins of the hot water bathhouse.

The Bodhi-tree Shrine: A Sacred Garden

Klaus Holzhausen

The Bodhi-tree Shrine or *Bodhigara* is not the only worship element in monasteries; it is omnipresent in all Buddhist temples in the country. Usually, a temple site is contains, besides the Bodhi-tree Shrine, at least three buildings: a stupa, an image house and a teaching or convention hall. The space surrounding these elements is sand covered, some with less and some with more plants or trees and integrated boulders. Often a pool with waterlilies is also part of the arrangement. The whole can be considered as a garden. It is not customary to view the modern Bodhi-tree Shrine itself as a garden or to describe it in such terms. However, it is a garden and not a building. Its ancestor was a roofless structure with a centrally placed tree.

> Buddhist teachings further promoted respect towards nature. The three important events of the Buddha - birth, attainment of spiritual enlightenment and passing away - were directly associated with trees. The Bodhi-tree under which Buddha attained spiritual enlightenment and supreme wisdom is sacred to Buddhists. A sapling (southern branch) of this sacred tree at Bodhgaya in India, brought to Sri Lanka in the 3rd century BCE and planted [...] at Anuradhapura, is still venerated by Buddhists as a supreme relic of the Master, and it is considered to be the world's oldest, recorded, living historical tree.[55]

A Bodhi tree (*Ficus religiosa*) at Anuradhapura, at the Mahavihara, has remained as a site of worship since the shrine was established in the 3rd century BCE, when a seedling or a shoot of the tree, under which the Buddha meditated, was brought from India. The very importance of this tree, with its

The Bodhi-tree Shrine at the Kelaniya Temple in the evening. These trees are highly venerated.

Next page, top and bottom: The oldest Bodhi-tree of the country has been growing for 2300 years at the Mahavihara at Anuradhapura.

Page 168, top left: Many of his most important branches are held up by high metallic supports.

Page 168, bottom: The archaic enclosure wall is probably one of the oldest constructed elements at the site.

Page 169, bottom right: An engraving from 1859 showing the Bodhi-tree in the 19th century.

THE BO-TREE AT ANARAJAPOORA.

2,300 years probably the oldest tree in Sri Lanka, has perhaps prevented scholars from gaining access to it for study. Little remains of the shrine buildings today save a sequence of high terraces around the tree and a few sculptures in modern image-houses. The probable oldest building, except for the tree and its walls, is the ancient high compound wall, endowing this sacred place with the character of a sand-covered courtyard.

Ancient Indian shrines were galleried structures allowing intimate access to the tree at higher levels. The Sri Lankan *bodhigara* was similar, consisting of a series of small walled terraces with a raised central platform for the tree. Entrance to the terraces was through doors or gates, cardinally oriented, and the shrines were square, circular or rectangular in plan. The largest is thought to be the *bodhigara* at the Jetavanarama, at Anuradhapura, whose terrace is 42 metres x 34 metres. The structures usually had tiled roofs supported by columns. The tiles were sometimes glazed in several colours or made of copper. The roof covered the terrace around the tree.

The whispering shade of the tree, contrasting with the bright white sand of the bare terrace and the often-white trunk, and the faint fragrance of incense, flowers and oil, impart to these gardens their mystique and ambience of quietude and shifting light and shade. The soft whisper of the leaves and the weight of the branches create a special kind of moving roof. A worshipper, compelled to walk around them, is confronted with an aesthetic found nowhere else.

In contrast, the Bodhi-tree terraces of the *giri* monasteries are often boulder and sand terraces with beautiful distant views.

Yatagala monastery in Galle is a fine example where the Bodhi-tree garden forms the upper-terrace, built in the middle of clusters of boulders which also act as the boundary wall, over which the sky and far vistas come into range of the devotee. Small individual boulders pierce the flat white sand floors overhung by the rustling foliage of the tree. The boulders and the patterns daily swept into the sand bring to mind the rock and raked pebble gardens of Japan.

Indeed, Yatagala is closer to the Japanese method of design because the small boulders appear to be artificially placed. In the Japanese tradition the entire landscape is artificial, whereas in Sri Lanka the site, views and natural landscape are integral to the design. The aesthetic traditions they invoke meld panoramic views of forests, mountains and lakes which accompany the choice of site. Conceptually, the spaces provide for both introspective ritual functions and an outward communing with infinite space.

Four cardinally oriented Buddha statues around the base of the tree originated in Mahayana practices. The act of watering the tree was one of the most meritorious a devotee could perform. The *Hamsa sandesa*'s haunting description: 'Salute with pleasure the Bodhi Tree as white as the celestial river straight and large of trunk which looks like lightening in a rain cloud because of its tender buds and blue foliage...',[56] attests to a delicate spiritual and aesthetic appreciation of nature. The Bodhi-tree ritual space is a highly designed garden form with an ancient genealogy that has, for centuries, reproduced spaces which foster a deep respect for silence and nature.

At the Yatagala monastery and temple the Bodhi-tree is situated on a boulder hill terrace, in the centre of a kind of natural boulder garden. Over the sand floor a number of smaller boulders are distributed, as in a Japanese temple garden. The whole constitutes a very beautiful example of a Bodhi-tree shrine.

This majestic Bodhi-tree is situated at Kandy, outside the main temple area, in the public park and near a Hindu temple.

The Colonial Encounter

Shanti Jayawardene
Klaus Holzhausen
Gianni Biaggi

Introduction

Sri Lanka's strategic position on the commercial maritime routes and the voracious European interest for land and resources account for the progressive colonisation of the island in the modern era. The meeting was unequal in terms of the British ability to mobilise military power and left a profoundly unbalanced physical and intellectual imprint on the island. Although the earliest colonisers were the Portuguese and Dutch, their access to the island was limited. They were unable to subdue the Kandyan kingdom whose capital lay somewhat protected by the dense forested mountain range of the central massif. In 1815, betrayal of the King of Kandy by his nobles gave the British possession of the entire island. British response to the Uva Wars of independence of 1817 was massacre and the total annihilation of the native aristocracy. The last war between the two peoples in 1848, completed British dominance. Violence underscored the colonial relationship which ended formally in 1948.

With the onset of the occupation of the island by Europeans, a major influence on gardens and landscapes arose from two sources: the importation of exotic plants from other regions of the world, and the introduction and development of large-scale commercial cinnamon, coconut, coffee, rubber and tea cultivation. Rather than encountering a *tabula rasa,* wherever the Europeans turned, they faced people with local knowledge of the land, its flora, fauna, history and culture. A large part of the colonial project was to access, collect and translate the archives of the colonised and take it to the heart of Europe for the advancement of Europeans. At the same time, European colonisers exported their own lifestyles and garden culture to the colonies modifying them to local conditions when necessary. Following ancient indigenous practice, the Portuguese and Dutch engaged in developing cinnamon and coconut plantations along the coastal belt. In 1769, Dutch Governor Iman Willem Falck grew cinnamon from seed in his botanic garden at Grandpass. Locals who processed wild cinnamon bark tried unsuccessfully to sabotage the trials by pouring hot water on the plants. But according to Swedish botanist Carl Per Thunberg, new plants were cultivated at Sitavaka, Kalutara and Matara. Native headmen were instructed to open cinnamon gardens.[1]

Early Colonial Dwelling Patterns

The Portuguese and Dutch colonialists and native elites, on their private estates, favoured dwelling forms with ample verandas and gardens which were partly based on indigenous models of *walawwas* manor houses. This domestic form represents one mode of exchange between indigenous patterns and baroque as well as neo-classical architectural elements and garden styles imported from Europe. The powerful, wealthy Azevedo, Albuquerque and Mascarenhas families of 1600-1700 Portugal are familiar names of ruling captain-generals in Portuguese colonial possessions such as the *Estado da India* and Ceilao. Their fabulously elegant *quintas*, large houses on country estates in wine growing regions of Portugal, are a testament to colonial wealth and suggest that the Portuguese contribution to similar country house dwelling types and gardens in Ceylon is possibly overlooked and unresearched.

The alternate court and royal palace which Captain General of Conquest, Azevedo, and his successors are believed to have maintained at Malwana from 1594 onwards[2], doubtless provided a splendid opportunity for developing a suitably complementary Luso-Lankan suburban architecture patronised by an ethnically heterogeneous dominant class who supported the Portuguese presence on the island. This is also largely true of their spacious town houses that await research. The expansive scale of Dutch domestic architecture in the suburbs of Galle included imposing entrance gates, pillared verandas and gardens containing the ruins of a swimming pool of huge proportions, recorded as the largest in the island in 1965.[3] Such sprawling built forms seem to owe more to the Portuguese *quinta* with its verandas, balconies and ornamental pools than to domestic architecture in Holland.

Sri Lankan-British Garden Forms

The period under British occupation gave rise to five main garden types which fused native and imported knowledge systems. Firstly, the botanic gardens and parks, of which *Peradenyia* is the most notable with its many different garden scenes in succession. Secondly, the bungalows and gardens on the large cinnamon, coconut and rubber estates, properties belonging to a landowning and entrepreneurial elite that flourished between 1860 and 1930, and a type that also possessed an urban variant. These seem to derive mainly from an imported or hybrid manor house or urban villa, probably evolved during the periods of Portuguese and Dutch occupation. The third type is the bungalow and garden developed on the tea plantations at higher altitudes. The fourth is the school garden, a striking example of which is the *Girls' School* at *Uduvil* in Jaffna. A fifth is the sports ground for golf, cricket, tennis, football, and horse racing. The most famous leisure ground is the popular Galle Face Green at Colombo which, created as a horse-racing ground, became a public park during the last decades of colonial rule.

Commercial Plantations

Under British occupation one of the most enduring and least commented upon results of the colonial encounter was the tragic loss of the rich extensive and heavily forested lands as well as peasant cultivated rice fields, medicinal groves, home gardens and royal and monastic flower gardens and orchards. Especially after 1817, land hitherto managed and cultivated by the people to serve their own needs was acquired by force and granted almost for free to a settler population. British actions resulted in a ruthless destruction of ancient land use patterns[4] and a monoculture and plantation economy serving British needs steadily replaced the older diverse economic and cultural systems. These massive land ownership transformations relied on the services of native ruling elements who sought to benefit from colonial rule.

Coffee plantations proliferated during the first half of the 19th century, followed by those for tea and rubber. To achieve this commercial goal the British completely disrupted indigenous economic structures. Having captured the land, numerous roads and railroad networks were built for swift movement of troops and transportation of the new plantation produce to the coastal regions. Driven to protect their profits, by the 1840s Britons recruited armed forces to control labour and prevent it leaving the plantations. In executing this transformation, the British inexorably modified the country's ecology. The steep landscapes of the magnificent forested high mountains were transformed into new views of regimented tea bushes and small 'Englands' with colonial built forms replete with bungalows, domestic gardens, tea factories and the unforgettable lines-homes for the indentured labour, the 'coolies', imported from South India, who worked under conditions of coercion, poverty and virtual servitude. During the 1868-1906 period, Europeans bought seventy per cent of the Crown land acreage sold in the Central Province – the primary coffee (and later tea) planting region in the country. Outside the coffee regions, natives purchased a greater share of the Crown lands sold.[5] The often-immense European-owned tea plantations were clustered in the mountain regions south-east of Nuwara Eliya and close to Adam's Peak. The bungalows built to accommodate Europeans evolved along the lines of Eurasian architectural models, as did their gardens.

Botanical Gardens

European collectors of exotic plants such as orchids brought a new kind of ecological danger to the colonies. Rapacious individuals denuded whole districts of forests as they shipped thousands of specimens back to Europe.[6] Botanical gardens feature impressively in Sri Lanka due to a British need to capture and advance 'scientific' knowledge to service the new plantation economies and triumph over their continental rivals in the construction of new scientific knowledge. In Sri Lanka under British occupation, the first of such gardens was the remodelling of a tract, developed by the Dutch, at Slave Island, Colombo, in 1812.[7] It was followed by a garden at Kalutara in 1817, Peradenyia in 1822, Hakgala in 1861 (an experimental cultivation station for chinchona, quinine) and Henarathgoda, Gampaha, in 1876 (an experimental station for rubber plants). The design and planting of the famous Peradeniya Gardens conjoins expertise of British officials and indigenous intellectuals, employed as subordinates in the colonial establishment. It was established on a site that belonged to the gardens of the Gampola Kings from around 1371.[8] The celebrated Daswatta royal garden of the Danakirigala temple, that supplied a thousand flowers for worship, is beautifully illustrated in the temple murals, as landscapes of trees in bloom (see Royal Gardens chapter).

The plantation owners with their European lifestyles and European gardens lived in a rough mountain solitude. Source: an old postcard, on display in a restaurant in the old city of Kandy.

Garden Houses

The British drew on the experience of the earlier colonisers and adopted a variety of shifting approaches to gardens and architecture whose morphology largely depends on how precisely the Empire evolved.[9] In late 18th-century Madras the Indo-British elites had developed a large spacious suburban dwelling type, outside the fort, where gardens were an important feature: they were known as garden-houses. The houses of the natives were notably larger than those of the outsider and displayed a sprawling suburban character. Their often single-storey flat-roofs and *chunam* plaster pillars mixed Anglo-Italian country-house traditions with indigenous elements [10] The need to travel into the fort daily, by palanquin and carriage, appears to have produced a characteristic feature of this dwelling type – the portico with a drive, encircling a central patch of lawn. The gardens of this dwelling type were noticeably part wild, densely planted with local flora including jasmine, mango, banana and guava and often contained a bathing facility.

The famous German naturalist Ernest Haeckel who visited the island in 1881-82, called his first morning at the Whist Bungalow in Colombo, his 'first morning in paradise'. Haeckel's host and then owner of the Whist Bungalow was Mr Stipperger, representative of the Austrian Lloyd Shipping Company in Ceylon. He purchased it from Sir Richard Morgan, a wealthy Burgher gentleman and acting Chief Justice of Ceylon, who had either planted or enhanced the garden. The house stood in front of the shore facing a fine expanse of water and the airy veranda commanded a view of the sea, the mouth of the river and a thickly wooded island. Haeckel experienced it as an enchanting spot containing specimens of almost every important plant flora of the island: 'it is thus not merely a pleasure-ground of blossoms and perfumes but an instructive botanical garden on a small scale'.[11]

> He was intoxicated by 'the palms, figs, bananas, acacias, and the terminalia laurels, myrtle, ironwood, breadfruit, and others, embraced and overgrown by gorgeous creepers, that endless variety of lianas which play so conspicuous a part in the flora of Ceylon [...] the broad-leaved Callas or Aroids, and the elegant ferns', above them rises 'the mallow, acacia, tamarind, Thunbergia, lilies and orchids'.[12]

Haeckel was impressed by both the variety and beauty of the native flora and the ecology of the rich gardens known as *gewattas*, which provided a symbiotic mixture of wild and cultivated plants using low inputs of labour and fertilisers, thus amazingly productive. However, Haeckel was not only a great naturalist and excellent scientific illustrator; he was also a talented painter. An example is his 1881 painting of the Weligama Bay. It shows a small rocky island in the bay. This is the island which the Count de Mauny Talvande purchased in the 1920s and transformed into a luxuriant garden, his *Taprobana*. But Haeckel also admired Charles Darwin and his theory of evolution, which led him to highly controversial ideas on race and eugenics.[13]

British impact on gardens in Sri Lanka

The sources of inspiration for more recent Indian and Sri Lankan gardens also look back to 18th- and 19th-century stylistic shifts in Britain. Designers such as Capability Brown and Humphrey Repton promoted large informal and picturesque parklands with clumps of trees to adorn estates with lavish mansions, set vast lawns with contorted beds of exotic flowers (brought into greenhouses and taken out in the spring: the practice known as *bedding out*), artificial lakes, statuary, streams, arboretums and impressive rock gardens. The 18th-century British stylistic preferences for parkland gardens, and the more formal Victoriana of Kew and the urban parks, which embraced extensive lawns, pools, fountains, bridges, artificial lakes, pagodas and flower beds with tree-lined walks, were. They also entered the gardenscapes of Sri Lanka.

The uniquely imperial European Arts and Crafts Movement which partly arose as a romantic aversion to the negative effects of industrialising Europe was imported across the globe. For imperial elites it harked back to the aesthetics of a cosy, safe, simple rural domesticity, far removed from the otherness of colonial places and the unease and violence of empire. Safety and familiarity balanced the coloniser status which was simultaneously alien, thrilling and threatening. Within the vast geographies and the forever unknowable secrets of the lands they governed, the coloniser intelligentsia struggled with rural nostalgia and the safety of a familiar private place called 'home'. The main exponents of the Arts and Crafts garden movement were the garden designer Gertrude Jekyll, often associated with the architect Edwin Lutyens, and the gardener William Robinson, author of the highly influential *The Wild Garden*. The style was developed for the new smaller properties ranging from the house to the club house, where the garden with a lawn persisted and a better connection between the house and the garden became possible. In high-altitude plantations, the old-fashioned cottage-garden became the paradigm. The beds were composed of shrubs and indigenous perennials arranged in subtly coloured *mixed borders;* garden rooms and pergolas set up on brick pillars appeared, set against the backdrop of the inevitable lawn, linked with topiary hedges of yew, dry stone walls and elegant steps. Imperial designers used colourful exotic plants, which at home were brought into greenhouses in the winter and taken out in the spring. In Sri Lanka, Peradenyia and Hakgala botanical parks are the best exemplars of the Victorian style, Roehampton Estate among others mirrors the Arts and Crafts ethos, while the Richmond Castle Garden presents an eclectic mix of Victorian, Anglo-Italian and Anglo-Indian styles.

During the late colonial period, in the 1920s-1930s, there appeared in Ceylon a talented amateur gardener, a Frenchman naturalised in Britain, Maurice Count de Mauny Talvande, who influenced the garden art through his writings[14] and through his own garden on the Taprobane island near Weligama. He contributed to prepare a new, more modern way of gardening after the independence (1948).

Atapattu Walawwa

The Atapattu Walawwa in Galle is a historical monument, a rare example of one of the earliest firmly datable (circa 1780 to '90s, the Dutch period) residential mansions in Sri Lanka. More than 200 years old, its authenticity and much of its original setting have been preserved. It is still owned and occupied by a direct, sixth-generation descendant of its 18th-century founder, who held the official post of 'Mudaliyar of the Atapattu of Galle'.[15]

A *walawwa* is built in the vernacular-manorial Sri Lankan style, with an admixture of European colonial elements and some well-integrated 19th century additions. The traditional domestic dwelling was a combination of enclosed glare-free and often thoughtfully ventilated internal spaces, open airy verandas and internal courtyards, an unshaded inner garden, with many potted plants and flowering shrubs, and a tree-covered outer garden.

Left:
The 18th-century's library building in the southern part of the garden.

Right:
The covered connecting walkway from the veranda to the library.

ATAPATTU WALAWWA

1 Main veranda
2 Living room
3 Inner courtyard
4 Kitchen and service rooms
5 Bedrooms
6 Dining room
7 Covered walkway to the library
8 Library
9 Formal garden in front of the library
10 Tree-filled parkland
11 Flowering beds
12 Western lawn
13 New houses and access drive
14 Kitchen garden
15 Northern valley and family cemetery
16 The inner slope of the west ridge
17 Buddhist temple and monk dwelling
18 Gateway and internal access drive
19 Southern valley
20 Lower Dickson Road

Drawing: Klaus Holzhausen, based on measurements on the site by the author
Source: Janaka Goonetilleke, *Atapattu Walawwa, Residence of the Gooneratne & Dias Abeyesinghe families of Galle*, 2012

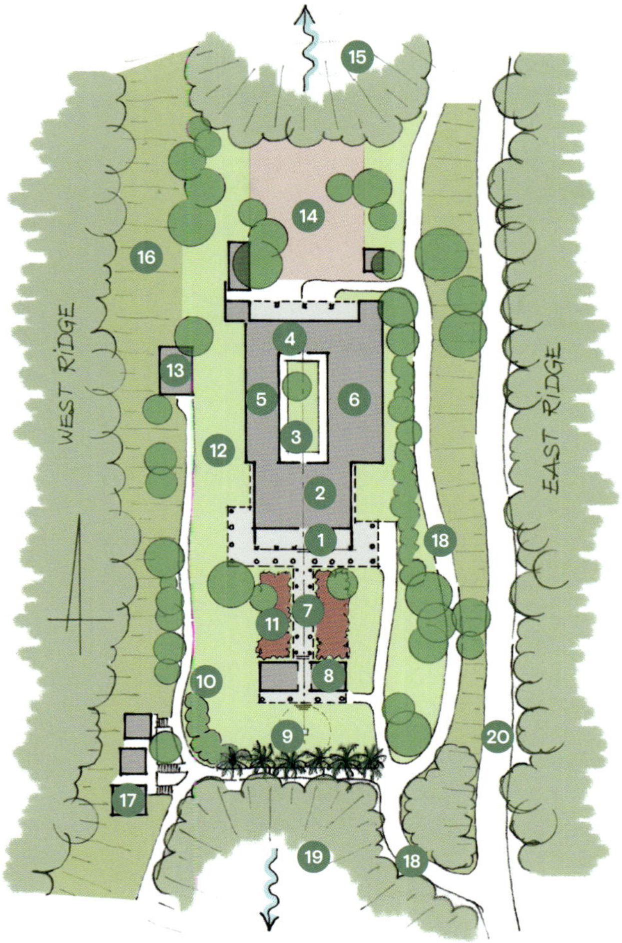

Set in an antique urban landscape, with a well-documented history, and of outstanding architectural quality, this urban villa still stands in its own authentic garden of 1.5 acres. The *walawwa* is situated on a saddle between two parallel ridges which run in a more-or-less north-south direction from the hinterland to the bay and harbour. Two valleys, behind and in front of the house, carry the rainwater in opposite directions, one leading inland, and the other flowing towards the sea.

The house is approached through a modest gateway and an internal drive, commencing in the south-eastern corner and running along the eastern façade to the rear kitchen garden, with branches to the main porticos (18). The garden design, only partly preserved, is still retrievable. It consists of several segments interlocked with the architectural layout:

- in front of the library (8) an almost entirely obliterated formal garden, today very simplified, centred on a marble bird bath (9);
- two small rectangular lawns, edged with two beds planted with flowering shrubs and perennials (11), and shallow drains on either side of the covered walk (7);
- the central courtyard (3) with a single jasmin plant and a stone basin in the middle of the grass-covered central space. It is rimmed by a stone flag bordered walk and a wide and shallow drain. Six key points are punctuated by stone slabs on which are placed stone basin stands;

The generous veranda is also a covered part of the garden; the many potted plants inside and ornamental bushes outside form part of the décor.

- a large lawn along the western side of the house and the library (12);
- a terraced hill side along the inner slope of the west ridge (16), now partly interrupted by new houses and an access drive (13);
- a small, tree-filled 'parkland' covering the south-western corner (10);
- the kitchen garden north from the house (14) and series of narrow terraces leading down to the north valley (15);
- the generous large verandas are adorned with many decorative potted plants, placed between the columns (1).

The particularity of this garden is that its traditional Sri Lankan character is preserved, with only minor European colonial influence. And the beauty of the penetration between the open parts of the architecture (veranda and covered walkway) and the flowers and foliage of the garden is touching and poetic. Other *walawwas* have been renovated and transformed into luxurious apartments or hotels. Where competent and sensible architects have been involved, the result can be splendid, also in terms of the gardens, like the Kandy House Hotel refurbished by architect Channa Daswatte.

The 'Royal' Botanic Garden, Peradeniya

The British colonial-instigated Botanic Garden Peradeniya has a rich history whose scope is scientific, economic, aesthetic and recreational. It takes its name from Sinhala Pera (guava) and Deniya (a plain). According to the Sri Lankan artist Laki Senanayake the 'Royal' in the title of the gardens presumably refers to the Kandyan royals who 'loitered therein in those days'[16], rather than to the distant patronage of the royal House of Hanover, in whose name the colony was ruled in the 1820s.[17]

The garden is located 6 km from the early modern capital Senkadagala, or Kandy in English, on a horseshoe-shaped peninsula skirted by the Mahaweli River. It is a slightly hilly plateau at an altitude of 460 meters, surrounded by steep slopes with a nominal forest cover. Since 1371 the park had been a royal pleasure garden, with the addition of a monastery and a *dagoba* at the end of the 18th century. The British sequestered the land in 1815. Pre-colonial markers are in evidence in the contemporary Japanese gardens. Under British occupation the new colonial garden was established in 1821, steered by superintendent Alexander Moon, who favoured coffee, cinnamon and other tropical plants of commercial value to the Empire. Many plants were brought to Peradeniya in 1821 from Slave Island in Colombo, a former Dutch garden, renamed Kew in 1812 by William Kerr. The garden received a firmer foundation in 1843, under superintendent George Gardner, who created an extensive herbarium. From 1849 it thrived under the stewardship of botanist George Thwaites and, thirty years later, under Henry Trimen. Its final form, however, appeared only during the first half of the 20th century.

From the time of inception of colonial gardens, British officers like Alexander Moon competed with European colleagues for possession of scientific knowledge in tropical botany. Moon's book *A Catalogue of the Indigenous and Exotic Plants Growing in Ceylon,* which compared, among other things, the Linnaean system of botany with the divisions of genera and species in use amongst the Singhalese in the English and Sinhala languages, was published in 1824. Unsurprisingly, Moon did not mention his closest aide, Harmanis De Alwis Seneviratne, although the book is a 'curious' hybrid work in both Sinhala and English script. It is not possible that Moon, who arrived after 1814, collected the vast amount of botanical data without help from native intellectuals. Local botanical and garden design knowledge was absorbed seamlessly by the colonial knowledge project. The present consensus with relation to all such joint colonial achievement is that it is both unequal and collaborative. Hence, the necessity

Top, from left to right:
The main entrance gate to the Peradeniya Botanic Garden. The generous ficus lawn with the araucaria walk in the background. In the vast lawn is growing a 70m-diameter ficus benjamina.

Middle:
A walkway through the glorious flowerbeds of the Victorian-style garden.

Bottom:
Cabbage Palm Avenue leading to the Great Circle.

The tempo of surprises at Peradeniya is rather slow and proceeds by light touches. Visual illusions are rare. In this extensive and typically English park, where a few rigorous axis interact with the predominant curvilinear paths, there is no suddenness; rather a gradual change of varied sceneries, an incitement to travel, to discover various cultures, styles and types of vegetation. The plateau with its gentle slopes is harmoniously nestled between the surrounding range of mountains. When crossing the long *ficus* lawn the view unfolds gently and the visitor is invited to go on. However, once arriving at the top of the plateau, he suddenly discovers the one major surprise: the wonderful appearance of the Mahaveli River.

Top:
The splendid Cuban Royal Palm Avenue.

Bottom left:
The so-called, Victorian-style Flower and Japanese garden.

Bottom right:
An artificial lake with the beginning of the bamboo collection in the background.

of moving beyond greatly exceeded the worth of any question raised on the issue.[18]

The 59 ha Peradeniya Garden, which includes 4000 plant species and cultivars, is the foremost in the country; two million people visit the park each year. Today it is an extensive English landscape garden, characterised by an alternation between large glades, walks and groves connected by a network of serpentine paths and tree-lined axes. The vegetation comprises individual specimens and collections, both native and exotic, grouped by area. After passing three imposing entrance pillars, we first see on the left, a walk lined with buttock coconut trees (*coco fesses*), native to the Seychelles, framing George Gardner's monument, a celebrative memorial in his name (a wink, perhaps, at the allegorical monuments in 18th-century English gardens?) and an unmistakable sign of a British colonial presence.

Nearby, a sweeping lawn surrounds a unique *ficus benjamina* tree 70 metres in diameter. Unfortunately, it has shrunk somewhat today, probably due to soil compaction by too many visitors; adjoining it is an *araucaria* (conifer native to South America and Australasia) walk. The concavity of the lawn makes it appear more majestic, since it has a greater variety of visual angles of incidence. Walking a little further through a typical Victorian garden, with flower beds framing a national herbarium building, the visitor arrives at the Great Circle, an impressive oval lawn and focal point of the park: it 'borrows' the hilly landscape surrounding it. Along its perimeter, memorial trees were planted by famous people. Here, too, was held the first rubber plantation fair. Beyond appears the *Cabbage Palm Avenue* (cabbage palm = Sabal palmetto), and close to it the splendid *Cuban Royal Palm Avenue* (Cuban royal palm = Roystonea reagia).

Turning back, one crosses a pergola with ornate white columns covered with queen's wreath (*petrea volubilis*), which leads to the orchid house. Here is a specimen of *grammatophyllum speciosum* – its habitat is another botanical garden, the Hakgala Park. It's a pity, however, as Mauny-Talvande writes, 'that some orchids were not let to grow in their natural state on trees'.[19] The most elaborate gardens in the park commence with the *Flower and Japanese Garden*. Here are on display, in a truly Victorian fashion, ribbon-coloured flower beds, rounded beds on the lawn and topiary trees, the whole contrasting with a tall, elegant sheaf-shaped palm tree against a mountainous backdrop. Following up above the river, on the west side, is a rock garden along an artificial lake; the Ayurvedic medicinal plant garden; the impressive and vast bamboo collection, another star attraction of the park; the palm and cycadas collection in which grows one of the largest palm trees in the world that emits a huge cream white inflorescence before dying; the pretty *students garden* shaped like an amphitheatre with many square beds; and the ebony and pine collection. The spice garden is located beside the exit.

At first glance, Peradeniya is a typical Victorian-style garden with a variety of contrasting groves and clearings, close subjects and long views. Finally, one appreciates its grouping of majestic trees and its dendrological importance, which makes it one of the foremost botanical gardens in the world. It is noteworthy that the strikingly unusual formations of tangled lianas draping trees, a characteristic of the wilderness ambience in hilly regions, is missing in the garden. Whether they deserve a place here as a type of 'forest' garden is an open question. The archaeological markers of the pre-colonial monuments and layout in the area of the Japanese garden are not presented to the public as such.

The Hakgala Botanic Garden

The Hakgala, the second largest park in the country, dates from 1861. It comprises 28 hectares located on a hillside at the foot of the huge Hakgala Rock facing the Uva Valley.
Hak-gala (meaning jaw-rock), lies at an altitude of 1750 m and is situated in the Nuwara Eliya district, in a nature sanctuary of the same name. The garden benefits from the two annual monsoons and a cool, humid and misty mountainous climate, with a mean temperature of 16 °C and a low of 3 °C. Trees of the whole world can grow here. According to a local tradition of the legend of the Ramayana epic, this was the pleasure garden where the demon King Ravana held captive the beautiful princess Sita. The garden is the work of English botanist George Thwaites, mentioned above. From the bark of the *cinchona* tree, he experimented on extracting quinine, a tonic used as a cure for malaria, and undertook experimental tea cultivation for the plantation estates nearby. The garden was developed in 1884 by William Nock, the new commissioner.

Today, Hakgala grows some 10,000 plant species allocated in ten areas, in a Victorian setting. Its attraction at the main entrance is a big, sloped crescent punctuated with pruned shrubs and stem trees, leading to a circular bed of *impatiens* and other annuals. Further up there are the spice garden, the fernery and the rock garden of 1921 where big blocks randomly arranged are anchored individually to the ground and overlook the lily pond. Other elements are: the arboretum with its particular pine trees native to New Caledonia; the orchid house surrounded by the tallest hardy orchid in the world – *grammatophyllum speciosum* already mentioned, which produces a spike 2.5 metres long; the rose garden with its hundred species on display in March and April; the cactus house; the patch of bulbs; long stretches and fields of agapanthus and clivias along small valleys; and the forest groves where grow majestic cedar and cypress trees. But of all these sites, the most enthralling is the fernery where dwarf and tree ferns intersect a maze of paths and brooks and thrive in the cool humid climate. Finally, there are many indigenous and migrating birds. Indeed, one does not expect to see this variety upon entering the park.

The botanic garden of Hakgala arose from the overlapping dual colonial projects of gathering useful knowledge and the civilising mission. It thus also served the importing and acclimatising of exotic plants and the experimenting of new cultures, such as tea. This jewel has evolved into something of a scientific Mecca and a natural site popular among visitors.

This page:
The main entrance to the Hakgala Botanic Garden with Victorian-style trimmed rhododendron bushes in flower.

Next page, top:
A beautifully located rock garden.

Next page, bottom left and right:
A carefully designed garden planted with a variety of shrubs and with a small pool in the centre.

One of the most impressive attractions at Hakgala is the fernery: the tree ferns thrive in the cool humid climate.

Two more views of the fernery at Hakgala.

Richmond Castle at Kalutara

Richmond Castle Estate is located south of Colombo near Kalutara. It is a majestic 4,200 square metre mansion, nestling in a 17.6 ha parkland adjoining the Kalutara River. It was built around 1907, in the Edwardian Italian style, with indigenous features tucked in. It belonged to a Sri Lankan notable, the Mudiyar Pabikada Mudali Don Arthur De Silva Wijesinghe Siriwardena (1871-1947), son of a wealthy and influential planter. The young Siriwardena studied in England and, on his return, the King appointed him a mudaliyar.

It is believed that the design of the elegant property was based on a palace in India, owned by Srirwardena's schoolfriend, Raja Rajeswara Sethupathi, the Raja of Ramnad, near Madurai, in the Madras Presidency. Three years after the construction of the house, Siriwardena organised a sumptuous marriage ceremony with Clarice Suriyabandara, but the marriage ended in failure due to the lack of children. He consoled himself for his loss by creating in the garden, south of the mansion, a group of sculptures of children facing the bedroom, while another group of female statues faces the opposite direction. When the marriage ended, Siriwardena chose to live as a hermit, residing in room Number 77 of the Queen's Hotel in Kandy, for the remainder of his life; he died in 1947. As stipulated in his will, today the property is an orphanage owned by the Public Trustee and open to the public. It is, however, in a poor state of preservation due to lack of funds.

The park of Richmond Castle had its own fruit and flower gardens and the owners often hosted banquets for dignitaries, both foreign and Sri Lankan and maintained a 50-man troupe of performers for the entertainment of guests. The Mudaliyar lived much like a provincial king, respected in the manner of the nobility.

The domain is entered through an impressive Roman-style, white-washed semi-circular gateway with

Bottom left:
The wedding photo of Siriwardena and Clarice.

Bottom right:
The neoclassical entrance gateway to the estate.

RICHMOND CASTLE

1 Access drive
2 Main building
3 Ballroom, theater
4 Entrance porch
5 Representative formal garden
6 Lower orthogonal garden with flower beds and pots
7 Service rooms and dwellings
8 Northern lawn

Drawing: Klaus Holzhausen, based on measurements on the site by the author

Top:
The southern, most representative front of the 'Castle' with the highly eclectic garden in the foreground.

Bottom left:
The elegant columns of the semi-circular entrance hall.

Bottom right:
The garden seen from the terrace on the first floor.

triple entrances. The gates are linked by a curving pergola with columns and the road ascends as a curved path framed by vegetation. A short drive, or if one prefers a long walk, up the gravel pathway decorated with curious marble statues and canopied in greenery, spotted by occasional bursts of colourful blossoms, leads to a spectacular first glimpse of the regal Richmond Castle: an elegant and opulent architectural gem that fuses different styles from the East and West.

The main façade is punctuated by neo-classical columns, loggias and balustrades and a triple pedimented façade in the eclectic Italianate style of the period. The entrance porch has an apse and columns. The space inside evokes an *Art Nouveau* ambience: the fine mouldings of the teak columns, the staircase with its cast iron balustrade, the stained glass windows with grape vine motifs. The castle features an intricate staircase with teak carvings, and 34 windows embellished with stained glass of exquisite design.

The most dazzling feature is the great ballroom and theatre, topped by finely chiselled teak trusses in a mixture of neo-gothic and Kandyan styles. It is said that an underground pathway system brings cool air from the nearby river beneath the banquet hall. There are sixteen rooms in total. The ceiling height is about 5 metres and the floor is supplied with natural ventilation, providing a welcome

freshness. The centre of the house is organised around a square courtyard in the native manner with a gravel finish, a central fountain and a few plants set in the corners. The rear section of the house is a single-storey wing also in the indigenous mode, with a spacious veranda with a central apse, perhaps originally functioning as private space. A large service wing borders one side of the rear garden, which is a sprawling large lawn framed by trees and a drive.

The front garden is an eclectic patchwork. Overall, it comprises a central lawn encircled by the road which, as stated earlier, is a typical feature of colonial garden houses of the 19th century and perhaps earlier. In the centre of this lawn stands a circular pool with a fountain in the middle of a set of four intersecting paths, more like the 15th-century Tuscan Villa Fiesole in Italy, than the *char-bagh* type pools of Sigiriya and the water channels of Persian, Timurid and later Moghul gardens. An embankment 3-4 metres high separates it from a second, rectangular parterre punctuated with the cast iron sculptures of women and children and vases painted white, and the circular design of an area that, like the vases, was covered with flowers. The main entrance path runs alongside the embankment in an elegant curve towards the entrance porch. Peculiarly, this path as well as the second parterre lie off balance on the left side of the mansion's axis, whereas on the right side, free-growing coconut trees and other plantings and a disused pool indicate a former cultivation. Notwithstanding the asymmetrical disposition and eclectic character, the whole exudes a certain unity due to the uniform whiteness of objects and the clear-cut limits between the garden areas and the variety of the plantings behind, framing the hills. The eclecticism and the huge dimension of the property indicate the desire of some sections of the elites to assert their power and wealth through architectural and garden design modes drawn from both British rulers and Indian Maharajas.

The exit from the property is fashioned along the curved path edged with cinnamon shrubs that descends and progressively tapers off the view of the edifice.

Top:
The second, rectangular neo-rococo parterre on a lower level, punctuated by white urns.

Bottom right:
The main access drive, lined by beautiful vegetation, runs in an elegant curve towards the entrance porch.

Roehampton Tea Estate Garden

Important elements of the today's hill country tea plantation landscape are the hundreds of the owners or managers bungalows and their gardens. Although witness to the violent colonial period, we should consider them also as a cultural heritage. After independence, and the departure of the British, mostly Sri Lankan Tea Companies became their successors. Many of the bungalows and gardens are now used by the new managers, others became part of the Tea Trail tourist programme and have been transformed into small luxury hotels, with serious consequences for their gardens.

The Roehampton Tea Estate domestic garden, created around 1910, is one of the few tea plantation gardens in private ownership and still largely in its original state. It is located between Haputale and Bandarawela at an altitude of around 1,400 m. It belonged to Lindsay Gordon and exudes an Arts and Crafts flavour. Maurice de Mauny-Talvande, who might have been involved in the design, published two undated pictures of the garden in his book *Gardening in Ceylon* (1921).[20] Originally, the estate comprised 3150 hectares, whereas today it is reduced to about 50. An access drive climbing up from the west leads towards the house in a large curve to arrive at a central portico. The typical tea estate bungalow has a hip and gabled roof covered with flat black tiles; the walls are rubble stone and semi-turrets with bow windows embellishing the corners. A path surrounds a circular lawn 38 metres wide, edged with *duranta* shrubs alternating with hortensias. Facing the portico, an opening with steps cut through a yew topiary to allow to reach the drive across the lawn.

To the south, truncated pyramid steps reveal, 2 meters below, a rectangular lawn parterre embellished by three pools, 95 cm deep, fed through a gully. The unusual shape of the pools resembles water lily leaves where each originates from six circle arcs (see detailed plan). The parterre is delimited on the east side by a *mixed border* flower bed and a rubble stone wall. It supports a long walk above, ending with a terrace and

ROEHAMPTON TEA ESTATE GARDEN

1 Access drive
2 Entrance porch
3 The Tea Estate bungalow
4 Sunken water and flower garden
5 Terrace viewpoint
6 Kitchen garden
7 Flower garden
8 Orthogonal lawn terraces
9 Circular lawn

Drawing: Klaus Holzhausen, based on measurements on the site by the author

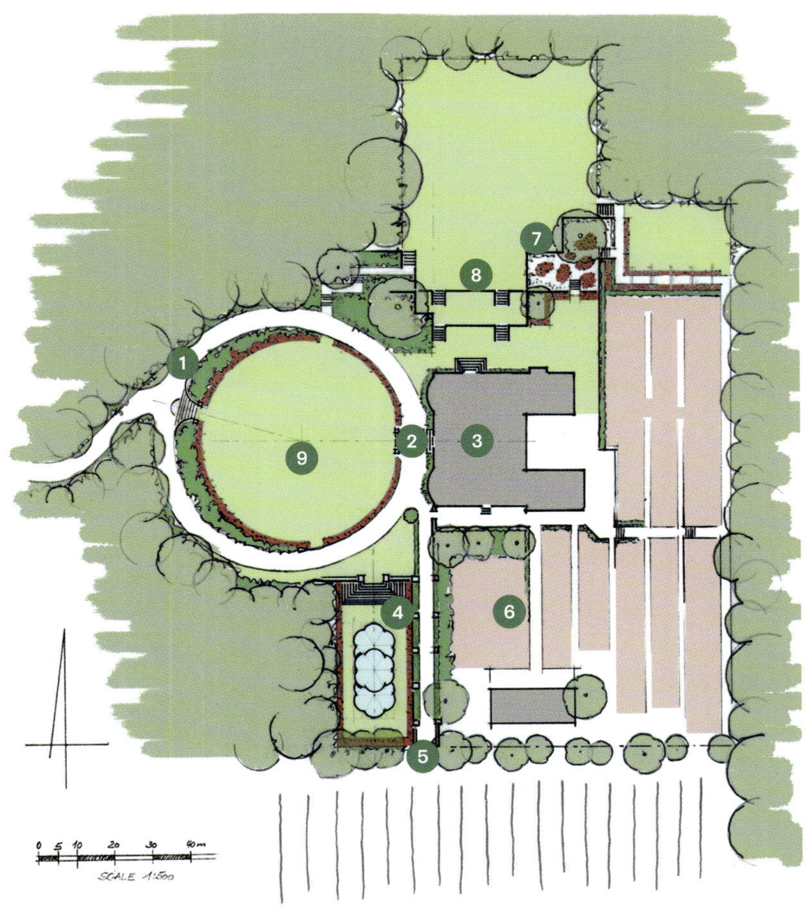

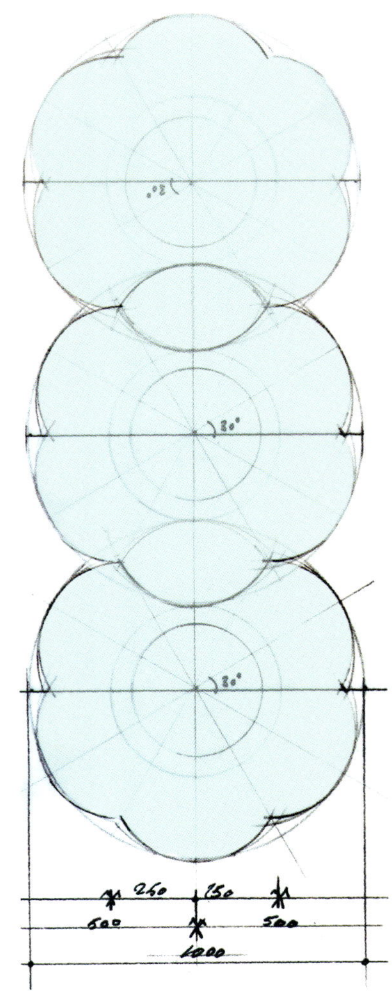

a pavilion, from which one can view the tea plantations beyond. Today it's an open sky walk bordered with *durantas,* but some old undated photos show a stone pillared pergola covered with climbing roses, a feature typical of Arts and Crafts garden design.

To the east of the house lie a large vegetable garden and an orchard scattered with flowers, which is visible through a trellis covered with *bignonias*: it is the utilitarian part of the property. Beyond grow dense trees framing the hills. On the north portion of the garden spreads a grassed jagged-shaped quadrilateral once occupied by a big pond. From here, the view of the mansion reads like tiered elongated horizontal planes. On the frontal plane, steps through small rubble stone walls open onto two lawn terraces which, in turn, lead to the ruffle stone walled house and its windows covered at the base by two strips of *ficus repens*, topped by the roof above. The geometric design of the two rectangular ornamental gardens, framing the big circle in front of the main façade, exerts a strong presence and contrast.

The whole has an alluring air of great simplicity and calm. It denotes a unity of style, forms, plantings and materials, while each sector offers a different expression. Thanks to the cool humid mountain climate this garden has a special non-tropical atmosphere. House and garden are both of great merit and in a good state of preservation. More research may uncover the involvement of professional garden designers at Roehampton, who worked in Ceylon under the banner of Arts and Crafts. At any rate, Roehampton undoubtedly evokes this style, even though the flower ornamentation, striking in the pictures of an earlier era, has now

Top left:
The Roehampton Estate bungalow seen from the circular lawn.

Top right:
A stairway short-cut leading to the circular lawn.

Bottom:
The Arts & Crafts flower- and sunken water garden, seen from the south and from the north.

Top:
The orthogonal lawn terraces and the bungalow seen from the north.

Bottom:
The Arts & Crafts flower- and sunken water garden shown in its original state in the 1920s. The historic photos are preserved inside the bungalow.
Photographer unknown.

disappeared. By chance, the garden is well documented in its original condition by photographs from the 1920s, which are conserved inside the house.

It is no accident that the sense of safety evoked by this cosy domestic Arts and Crafts style arose in the era of high imperialism. There was a harsh side to the lonely lives led by European planters, self-exiled in foreign lands. Often disease was their companion in huge isolated windswept bungalows, on hill tops, surrounded by people whose land and resources they took by force. Injustice mars the pleasure of those elegant high teas, still served on the exquisitely tailored lawns of the hill country bungalows. The now sterile mountain landscapes of commercial crops hide the dark side of greed. Behind the legacy of the part alien cosy domestic gardens, epitomising the British planter life, rests the history of destruction of a people, their lives and their natural environment.

The Girls' School at Uduvil

Located north of Jaffna, this girls' school compound is nestled in the countryside near Uduvil. It represents colonialism and the tradition of Christian mission schools in the country and was established in 1824 by American missionaries on the remains of an abandoned Portuguese Franciscan mission. One of the oldest boarding schools in the country, its goal was to promote Western Christian notions of education among young women at a time when illiteracy was rampant. The girls who were admitted in the early years came from poor families and mostly lacked a solid European culture, just as Europeans were equally illiterate in terms of indigenous culture which they had decided was 'primitive' and had to be eradicated. 'Truth shall make you free' is the school's motto. We might ask what precisely is this 'truth' from the point of view of a colonised person? Today, the school caters for 1,330 girls from age 5 to 18, from the first grades to the High School diploma.

This charming old building dating from the Portuguese period today accommodates the school offices.

Next page, top:
The surroundings of the entrance porch are full of potted plants, vines and ornamental shrubs.

Next page, bottom left:
Inside the loop of the access drive is a charming, small but luxuriant garden.

Next page, bottom right:
The modern library, visible in the background.

EN 8700

The whole site is articulated on a rectangular grid of one- or two-storey buildings alternating with garden courtyards akin to low-rise housing. The colonnaded central nucleus with its entrance porch, crossed by the looped access path evokes the approach to similar colonial estates such as Roehampton, the difference being that here the space inside the loop is a luxuriant garden. The striking generous spatial layout and proportions of the building indicate that it might be an adaptation of a 16th-century Portuguese construction. It contains the principal's residence and an annexe upstairs for guests. This elegant building faces the ornamental garden with a pergola of thin masonry columns holding up a metal covering which recalls the colonial period. This gem, with its opulent plantings, flanked by enormous, densely growing trees, greets

Between the different school buildings are courtyard gardens, planted, to varying extents, under the shadow of trees, with sandy floors, some with decorative fountains.

Apart from sports grounds, in some courtyards there are also vegetable gardens cultivated by the children. Gardening and vegetable cultivation are part of the learning programme.

visitors at the entrance to the compound. Wandering through the estate, one discovers several 19th- and 20th-century classroom pavilions, namely a science building with its accommodation; other housing units with galleries above; a chapel whose columns have Neo-Egyptian capitals and a Neo-Gothic church; a big theatre auditorium; and a series of garden courtyards. The whole becomes an intertwining between buildings and gardens which creates a visual transparency with a sense of depth. The in-between garden spaces are richly planted with trees, shrubs, and ground cover, punctuated by decorative fountains and meshed with walks and paved areas where sports are practised. Some of them are partly used as vegetable gardens, where children learn the basics of gardening. In the dry seasons the ground cover mostly disappears and a gravel surface emerges changing the lush green character of the trees and the vivid colours of the flower gardens. Throughout the year, the variously planted spaces interact with and enhance the general lightness of the pavilions.

This example stands for many other private schools in Sri Lanka with a comparable tradition whose gardens are a product of coercion integral to colonial cultural transformation even if there were repressive aspects to female life in Ceylonese culture as well. Missionary school structures helped enforce change of the native moral order all over the Empire. What we may consider as the quite magnificent garden estates owned by these famous schools are indeed subtly inflected by the darkness inherent in their very conception.

Taprobane at Weligama

The period of British colonial occupation of Ceylon gave opportunities for some Englishmen to indulge their fancied garden design talents during the early 20th century. Maurice Talvande was born in France to a well-to-do family although his father, a banker, lost his money. Talvande was educated in England and married Lady Mary Byng in 1898. The marriage gained him access to royal circles through her family connection with Queen Victoria. He may have become an exile due to rumours of homosexual tendencies, bankruptcy and the small stipend granted by his wife. Talvande usurped the title of Count de Mauny Talvande, a title which had been granted by Napoleon to the French politician Clément de Ris. Talvande was invited to Ceylon in 1912 by Sir Thomas Lipton, a Scotsman who had made a fortune selling Ceylon tea. He and Lipton belonged to the local European circles.[21] In 1925 Talvante purchased the island off Weligama Bay, which he called Taprobane, the ancient Greek name for Ceylon. Talvante comments: 'I found the spot of ideal beauty which would fill my dreams and keep me there for the rest of my life.'[22] In Weligama he founded a successful furniture design and manufacturing business in which he had also a creative role, but which unfortunately fell victim to the Great Depression in 1930.

The island site which Talvande purchased was a bare, abrupt outcrop of rocks which he transformed into a luxuriant garden, his private Eden, covered by some 800 species of trees vines, and shrubs, meandering paths joining panoramic viewpoints and a spring. On the summit he built an octagonal house in Neo-Palladian style inspired by precedents in Capri and the Vatican gardens whose furniture he reproduced. The carefully planted atmospheric terraces and loggias speak both of Italy and Ceylon. In describing its south side, he said: 'There was nothing between me and the South Pole.'[23] Alas, his estate has today turned into a luxurious renting facility.

Maurice Talvande wrote two books, *Gardening in Ceylon* (1921) and *The Gardens of Taprobane* (1937). In both he displays his talent as a gardener and horticulturalist rather than as landscape designer, giving many details on the cultivation of plants, their evolution, the type of soil, the climate, but without laying out a pre-established programme. Indeed, he draws no plans of his garden at Taprobane or of the colonial estates for which he lavished advice on their owners – Roehampton, Netherleigh and Leefe in Colombo – and the photos of them are undated. Nonetheless, one can sense that he had a definite penchant for Arts and Crafts rather than Victorian gardens, for he declares towards the end of his second book: 'The flower

Top left:
Portrait of Maurice Count de Mauny Talvande by David Paynter, early 1930s.

Bottom left:
The island in Weligama Bay, painted in 1881 by the German biologist and explorer Ernst Haeckel, before Maurice Talvande purchased it. Source Rohan Pethiyagoda, *Pearls, Spices and Green Gold, an illustrated history of biodiversity exploration in Sri Lanka* 2007, p. 149

Top right:
The Taprobane island today.

Bottom right:
Maurice Count de Mauny in the late 1930s, some years before his death in 1941. *Photographer unknown.*

bedding phase has given way – except in the formal gardens – to a more artistic herbaceous border, and even that is only a step towards true art which is to be found in the wild garden, because it works hand in hand with Nature and brings out its effects while it aims at simplicity which is the quintessence of art.'[24] A nature-oriented approach in garden art rather than an artificial one.

His two books may have influenced the way gardens were planted and maintained in Ceylon. And a few decades later Bewis Bawa had praise for him. On the one hand, Talvande was an opportunist, and his avaricious and ostentatious personality was evident when, for instance, he wished to 'lavishly decorate the Weligama beach with lighted coconuts and hold a procession of dancers and fireworks at the local taxpayers' expense'.[25] His attitude somewhat reflects the larger picture of British colonial society's self-centred outlook towards the tradition of indigenous Sri Lankan garden art. On the positive side, Talvande was a talented and prolific gardener and planter with eclectic views.

1 See Moonesinghe 2017.
2 Biedermann 2014, 64.
3 Brohier 2000, 188.
4 Moldrich 2016, 7.
5 Bandarage 1982.
6 Herbert 2011, 179.
7 Rosen 2016, 283.
8 Sujit Sivasundaram, Islanded, Kindle, loc 3010-25 of 8888.
9 See Herbert 2011.
10 Jayewardene-Pillai 2007, 159.
11 See Haeckel 2008.
12 Ibid.
13 Brunner 2017.
14 Talvande 1921; Talvande 1937.
15 Mudali (or Mudaliyar) was a colonial title and office in Ceylon (now Sri Lanka) which was part of the native headman system. The Portuguese colonials created the Mudaliyar class in the 17th century by enlisting natives of different castes from the coastal areas. The Dutch continued the practice of the Portuguese. This class used the Mudali as a hereditary title, however the British re-established a Mudaliyar class, with appointments that had the title of Mudali, this process was stopped in the 1930s when the Native Department of the British government of Ceylon was closed down.
16 Lewcock 2014, 31.
17 Sujit Sivasundaram observes that a recent guide to the Peradeniya Botanic Garden describes its rich history 'in a way that no European history has ever done'. (Sivasundaram, Kindle, Loc 3025 of 8888)
18 Lahiri 2015, 17.
19 See Talvande 1921.
20 Cave 1921.
21 Aldrich 2018, 68.
22 Talvande 1937.
23 Ibid.
24 Talvande 1921.
25 Talvande 1937.

The Cuban Royal Palm Avenue at the Peradeniya Botanic Garden.

A beautiful encounter between modernism and tradition, between the current infinity pool at the Kandalama Hotel and the ancient man-made Kandalama Lake landscape.

Modern and Contemporary Gardens

Shanti Jayawardene
Klaus Holzhausen
Gianni Biaggi

Introduction

From the 1940s, the gardens conceived by Ceylon's elites revisited and retrieved design traditions which were not quite 'lost', but – more accurately – erased and suppressed with the loss of patronage and status during colonial occupation. This phenomenon of erasure was both physical and visible in the narratives of the 'civilising missions' of European rulers and of the national elites.

The masterpieces created by Bevis Bawa, at *The Brief*, from the 1940s, and his brother Geoffrey Bawa, at Lunuganga, since 1957, point towards the recovery or reimagining of aspects of those lost traditions. The Bawas were skilled designers (Bevis was a self-taught garden designer, Geoffrey a trained architect). They encountered many cultures during their travels overseas and freely blended diverse kinds of design knowledge with the great traditions of the island.

Geoffrey Bawa is best known for his architecture in which the buildings are closely interwoven with gardens and water features. He reinterpreted the garden schemes of the traditional domestic house, 'opening the house out into the garden and bringing the garden into the house'. He took great care in selecting plant material, especially the bold use of foliage plants. His thirty-year encounter with Lunuganga, the elaborate riverside garden complex he fashioned around his country house at Bentota, epitomises these interests. In his later and more formal projects, as much as in many parts of Lunuganga itself, he combined trees, water, garden areas and architectural spaces in an approach often recalling the garden landscapes of Anuradhapura, Sigiriya and Polonnaruwa, but in an entirely fresh and modern way. His courtyard water gardens are amongst his most original creations, yet they fit easily and perfectly in a continuing Sri Lankan tradition.

This is even more emphatically the case with the next generation of garden creators, who shaped Diyabubula in Dambulla and the Boulder Garden Hotel near Kalawana, where the wheel turns full circle, and the boulder and forest gardens find purely modern – yet perennial – expression.

The complete liberation of form, within a given framework of topography, flora and history, marks modern Sri Lankan gardens, as much as it distinguishes the boulder and terrace gardens of early historic times.

Bevis Bawa's Gardens

Oh, would some Power give us the gift
To see ourselves as others see us!
(Robert Burns)

'Oh, but how preferable if by some magic spell
others can see us as we see ourselves'
(Bevis Bawa)

Bevis Bawa (1909-1992), a disarming, jolly and slightly impish lanky person about two meters tall, was a man out of the ordinary with a great sensual creativity. He was the son of wealthy parents of mixed Sri Lankan-European origin. His father was a famous lawyer and may have belonged to a Muslim family with antecedents in Beruwela. His mother's Dutch burgher family, the Schrader's, owned a low country plantation, the Kimbulapitiya, in the Negombo hinterland, with a comfortable house and a big richly planted garden, where the brothers often spent their weekends. His brother Geoffrey (1919-2003), became a renowned architect. After the Royal College, in 1929 Bevis Bawa joined the infantry, and became aide-de-camp to several colonial governors of the country.

He was also a talented raconteur, draughtsman, unusual cartoonist, sculptor, garden designer and a traveller in the family tradition. In 1922 he accompanied his parents to England; in 1934 he travelled to China, Japan and other Asian countries; in 1946 to India. In 1949 he returned to Europe for a *Grand Tour* of ten months, and in 1958 he returned to Japan. The trips clearly influenced the mixed Eurasian language of his works, guided by his personal intuitive aesthetic.

From the early 1930s Bevis was expected to manage the rubber plantation *The Brief*, 10 km east from Bentota. In 1949 he inherited it from his mother, but his interest in gardening and landscaping had already began much earlier.

The Brief Garden: A Mirror of Bevis

The Brief was an 80 ha rubber plantation. From 1949 Bevis began to realise his ideas and to convert it into an enchanting garden with a bungalow, but At the end he was only able to retain five hectares due to insolvency. Removal of the rubber trees and the opening up of views from the bungalow to the west, comprised the first phase of transformation. Over a long period, he laid out a number of beautiful landscaped, colourful and densely planted spaces. In 1956 the Australian artist Donald Friend came to stay until 1962. During this time the now beautifully planted garden received an artistic boost as the two creators worked well together. Bevis sculpted from Friend's drawings. Throughout the garden this successful collaboration is evident in the paving stones, the anthropomorphic vases, a Bacchus bird bath, fantastical heads and other sculptures.

The garden, sloping onto a terrain surrounded by dense vegetation and to the west by rice paddies, contains a series of 'rooms' or spaces that are intimate, introvert and pluricultural. It brings together various atmospheres which interact with the surrounding landscape. Diverging curved paths criss-cross a lush vegetation of more than 500 native species. The garden rooms, shady retreats, nooks and inviting alcoves appear to make it seem larger than it is. The embankments follow the contour levels to generate a garden of paradoxes, allusions and illusions, reflecting its creator.

The eastern access road arrives at a roundabout, where two pillars representing Pan-like male figures frame a long palm avenue. They lead the visitor to a courtyard which gives access both to the towering bungalow, dissimulated by a gate, and to a narrow and contorted walk that directs him to the garden proper. On the way appears a handsome, rounded ceramic decorated bench, then the *turtle fountain* nestles below. Above the embankment slope there finally emerges a metal umbrella-shaped roof shelter: it is the starting point of a narrow stepped trapezoidal waterfall slowing down the perspective effect; it is lined with bamboos and ends with a sculpted fountain of a jocular boy peeing, just like the Manneken-Pis in Brussels. Pointing slantwise towards the bungalow, it seems to approach it (see drawing). This arrangement is strangely reminescent of the waterfalls in the French garden of the Foundation Ephrussi-Rothschild at Saint-Jean-Cap-Ferrat. On carrying on up the grassy slope all around, an opening in the bamboos reveals suddenly below a long neoclassic staircase ending at a circular pool. Finally, on reaching the flat lawn around the bungalow, a third visual axis is revealed falling on a trapezoidal lawn parterre which frames a view of the landscape beyond. Here, west of the house, the garden fans out in three directions inviting the visitor to follow them.

THE BRIEF GARDEN

1 Arrival avenue
2 Arrival court, entrance
3 Terrace with pergola
4 Veranda
5 Spanish garden
6 Moon gate and open air bathroom
7 Water terrace and water steps, framed by an avenue of bamboo
8 Flight of neoclassical steps, water lily pond
9 Japanese miniature ornamental garden
10 Pavilion and bird bath
11 The expansive lawn and an Indo-Grecian horse
12 Party place and pavilion

Source: *The Architectural Heritage of Sri Lanka. Measured Drawings from the Anjalendran Studio*, David Robson & Dominic Sansoni, 2016 Laurence King Publishing Ltd., p. 198. The drawing has been adapted by the author

Top left:
Following the walk from the gate into the garden, the first two carefully sculptured 'folies' appear, a fountain and an elegant bench, perfectly integrated.

Bottom left:
The long, stepped trapezoid cascade, running down to the metal umbrella. The space is framed on both sides by bamboos.

Top right:
The same cascade, looking up to the sculptured fountain, source of the water. The optical illusion makes the water stairway appear to have the same width from the source to the bottom.

Bottom right:
A classical stairway leads down to a circular pond surrounded by luxuriant vegetation.

Behind a huge frangipani tree, thanks to verandas and pergolas, house and garden interpenetrate.

Rambling down to a lawn area the visitor first comes across a Hindu-Greek horse sculpture and two Portuguese urns, then a small Japanese garden decorated with a lantern and a miniature Chinese pagoda. At the opposite end, a flight of steps leads to a Buddhist lunar stone. Below, two barbecues and a rectangular pavilion are also provided, where the useful and the beautiful meet. Following another path from this game area, the stroller ascends to the circular pond, and climbing the flight of classical steps and following the cascades upwards, arrives on the lawn surrounding the bungalow. But the surprises are not yet finished. The house is a series of flowing spaces with sober furniture and inside–outside relations of high quality, opening up through picture windows to pergolas and to the main western garden, as well as to two unexpected small enclosed gardens. One is the *bathroom garden,* where a door painted in blue opens onto a lavatory; from here, a Chinese gate leads to the main garden. The other one is the *Spanish garden* east of the house, a Spanish patio with a central four-lobed pool leading into an alcove equipped with a shower, a mirror and a grotesque head spouting water.

The tour is completed, as a kaleidoscope. Having accessed the property and walked along the path, the garden bursts out, revealing its many-faceted art works and fascinating plant associations. On the one hand, the *Brief Garden* is an eclectic microcosm which nonetheless has a unity and a beautiful harmony; on the other, from a horticultural and botanical point of view, it is one of the most interesting gardens in the country.

Today, since Bevis Bawa's death, *The Brief* belongs to Dooland de Silva, who was Bevis's chief gardener, and who has become himself a well-known landscape architect. He maintains the garden following the instructions and the spirit of his former master.

We find here an intentional concentration of both illusions and surprises within a relatively confined area. The senses are on the alert at every moment, the unexpected greets one at every corner. The general aim is playful. But the surprise starts as one arrives unexpectedly in front of the gate of the estate, for this place lost in a forest is not easily found.

Surprise manifests itself at all scales: from leaf patterns, paintings and drawings by Laki Senanayake, panels of terracotta, tiles, polished jars, rough Chinese pottery and other grotesque heads and waterspouts by Barbara Sansoni and Donald Friend, to landscape features and atmospheres where light and shadow follow one another through lush vegetation, where space alternately expands and contracts. For this is a work of art where painting, sculpture, craftsmanship, plants, pathways and landscape converge to convey a unified concept.

Perhaps one of the most striking features is the trapezoidal waterfall that alters its natural perspective, a unique and rare example found in landscapes.

Two jars mark the transition from the main garden to the eastern rectangular lawn.

BRIEF GARDEN, WATER STAIRWAY

Detail drawing

Drawing: Gianni Biaggi, based on on-site measurements by the author

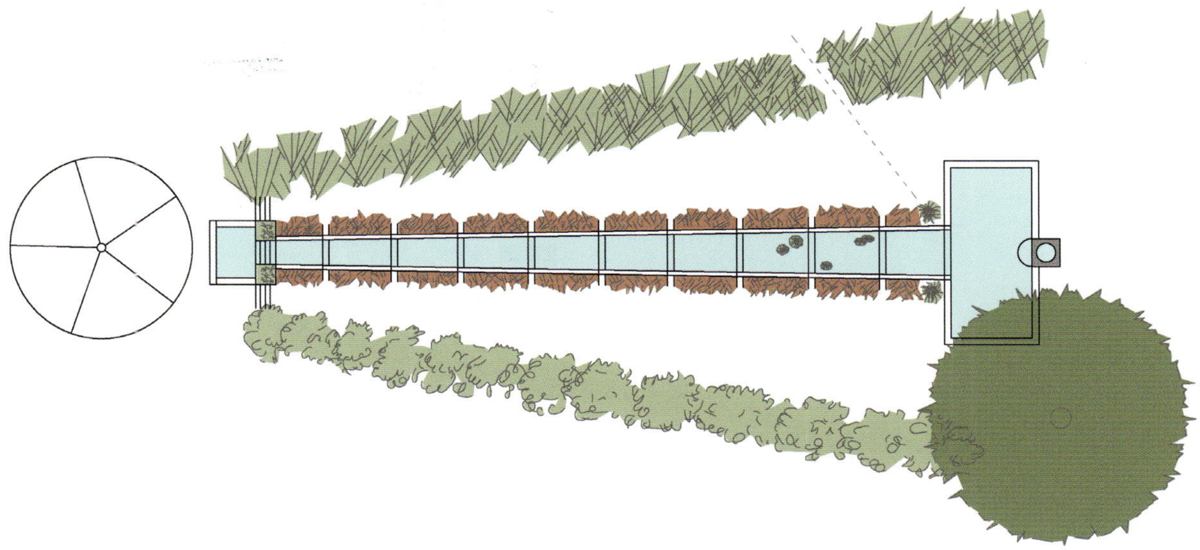

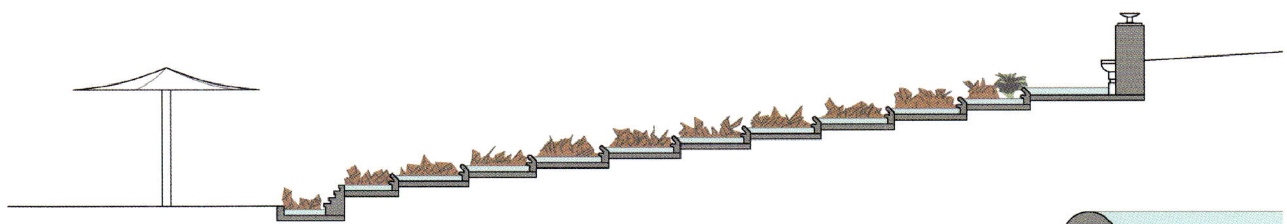

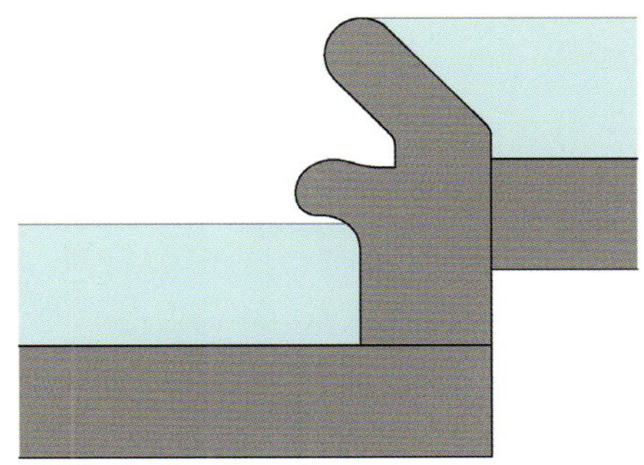

Bottom left:
An opening to the east gives the garden a view over the landscape.

Bottom right:
Many of the concrete slabs are decorated with imprint of leaves from the garden's trees.

Previous page:
A Chinese moon gate between the main garden and the bathroom garden.

The Gardens of the Sigiriya Village Hotel (the older part)

With his knowledge and the experience of his own garden, Bevis Bawa began to offer a consulting service in landscape architecture.

Convincing examples of his talent as a landscape architect are the gardens of the Sigiriya Village Hotel, which he realised in the 1980s.

The rooms of the hotel are organised in groups or rows of small cottage houses. Every two rows form a generous garden space, each one dealing with a particular theme. A few large old trees have been conserved, so that they generate a strong third dimension, shadows and a pleasant atmosphere.

In essence, the design of all the garden spaces is organic, which makes a difference with the second, more geometric part, designed by Laki Senanayake later in the 1990. The different themes are:

- a miniature countryside ambiance with a rice paddy field, water channels and a kitchen garden, surrounded by fences and bushes and some large trees;
- straight walkways punctuated by agaves, an open, moulded lawn, in the middle of which is a huge tree framed by a square low wall, like a *Bodhigara* or bo-tree;
- a succession of different ponds in hollow ground, islands around pre-existing trees in the ponds, fish, turtles and other animals;
- several ponds connected by cascades, water overflowing from one pond to the next lower pond, the whole is like a stream.

The entrance areas near the houses are colourful and densely planted with a rich palette of tropical plants. The arrival and reception area of the hotel is dominated by a big organic lotus pond with an important tree-grown island. Strolling through all these very well-maintained gardens is an amazing sensual pleasure.

The different garden spaces between the rows of cottages each deals with a different theme.

Top left:
A miniature countryside ambiance with paddy (rice) fields.

Top right and middle left:
A relatively open and generous sunken lawn, interrupted in the middle by a large tree surrounded by a low square wall.

Middle right:
A more wooded space with organic design and an artificial river as focal point.

Bottom:
An artificial lotus pond with planted islands in front of the hotel reception.

Geoffrey Bawa's Gardens: from Kimbulapitiya to Lunuganga

A country home on ancestral lands was the birthright of the Kandyan elites. It symbolised ancient blood and hereditary wealth. The Bawa family belonged to the nouveau riche professional groups in the south. They often acquired status by buying land and accumulating titles bestowed by the British. Geoffrey Bawa's father lacked a rural base. It was common for those with land to possess several homes in addition to a Colombo mansion, a rural mansion and vacation homes in the hills.

From the early 1930s Geoffrey Bawa's brother Bevis was expected to manage the rubber plantation *The Brief*, in semi-rural Bentota, which belonged to his mother. Geoffrey Bawa purchased his country estate at Lunuganga, a rubber plantation with an old house, in Bentota, in 1948 as a young man 29 years of age. The work of transforming this into his country home began in earnest after his return from London in 1957 as a qualified architect at the age of 38. Along with a new architectural practice, and a new library with a supply of books on historical European gardens, Bawa started creating his own garden at Lunuganga. Today, the garden is 10 hectares in extent. There are different opinions as to whether the garden designs owe more to European rather than the classical traditions of indigenous gardening.

Bawa's maternal family were Schraders, part of a burgher elite that acquired land in the south when colonial laws disrupted older landholding patterns. The Schrader families were planters whose Kimbulapitiya homes were set amid cinnamon and coconut plantations. The Bawa family plantation possessed a house and garden, built most probably by Mrs Bawa's father Frederick Justin Schrader. Mrs Bawa often took her sons to spend weekends with her brother Frederick Alexander, who inherited the Kimbulapitiya estate.[1] Bawa remembered how 'marvellous it was, sitting on the long verandah after lunch having endless conversations of limited interest…'[2] The house and garden may be provisionally dated to a time between 1850-1900. In contrast, Bawa's cousin Ronnie, his Uncle Fred's son, inherited wealth, lands and the ancestral Schrader home.

Today, the house is fronted by a garden on a small hillside, once richly planted, of which now only an evocative skeleton remains. It is composed of a series of narrow terraces separated from the house by an entrance drive, almost encircling the terraces, as it rises to the portico. The terraces repeat the ancient landscapes of the undulating rice paddies of the hill regions and were probably finished with pressed earth, gravel and/or wild grass. The dense verdant garden, within the flat repetitive landscape of the coconut plantations, is a surprise, as are the sudden changes of level, shade and the unusual flora. Glimpses of water in the distance would have enhanced the sense of wilderness. The absence of clipped lawns and the lineaments of the majestic trees along the terraces, some still tangled in lianas and spilling vines, conjure up a sylvan magic from the past. On a more prosaic note, the trees bear evidence of an interest in plants and an eye for a particular aesthetic. Careful selection achieved the enchanting, wild ambience of the original designer. Large jars, pots and Shanghai baths hid among the luxuriant foliage.

Among the many varieties of trees are the double araliya – the main feature on the northern terrace at Lunuganga – clumps of fine bamboo, diva, kitul, mango and pandanus. The garden merges with the larger landscape of the plantation and distant views. It has two small water features: an elliptical pool fed by rainwater from the roof is connected by a sinuous rill to a circular bath set in a lower terrace; another shallow pool has a fountain at its centre. The precise contours of the gardens imagined, built and planted by an older generation of Schraders, and their fleet of gardeners cannot be traced. Nonetheless, Kimbulapitiya cast its shadow on the memories as well as the present of the Bawa brothers. They may have been inspired to resurrect the environment of their grandfather's home in their new country houses.

While Kimbulapitiya has none of the subtle finesse of the boulder and sand terraced gardens, also typical of *giri* monasteries, the absence of rolling lawns and that pulling back in time seem to set the Schrader garden within a non-European spatial and aesthetic conceptual domain. It is not stylised like *The Brief*. It brings Lunuganga into focus.

Lunuganga

Geoffrey Bawa wrote that Lunuganga was always meant to be a 'garden within a garden, an extension of surroundings' where the landscape is large in scale. Green is the colour of the landscape, 'the greatest beauty being the sun filtering through leaves'. There are hardly any flowers other than wild hibiscus, ipomea, jasmine, and allamanda giving an occasional pointillist moment of varied colour against the background of green.[3] His comments recall the 18th-century English landscape gardens of William Kent who used the site to make winding paths, streams, and views, designed to set off the Palladian architecture he admired. Landscape gardens in 18th-century England were 'the product of cosmopolitan taste, a classical education, a Grand Tour and a familiarity with fine art.' Enclosures, in the early part of the century and between 1760 and 1780, resulted in many large undeveloped estates which speeded the spread of the new fashion for landscape gardening. To re-create the living landscape as a 'Platonic ideal, in a "chastened or polished" form, was of course expensive, and another sign of exclusivity.' It was 'always a visual' and at times literal appropriation of 'private and common land for aesthetic reasons' that reflected the real changes wrought by enclosure.[4]

Overall, Lunuganga had much in common with regard to the material foundations of landscape gardening and the picturesque in England. It was expensive, exclusive, and represented the cosmopolitan tastes of the owner. A garden laid out according to the landscape theories of the Picturesque requires the composition of the landscape scenery into a picture with a 'beautiful' foreground that is geometrical for human use; a middle ground (picturesque park) that is a serpentine park in the manner of Lancelot Brown; a (sublime) background that is natural scenery as little affected by man as possible. The foreground at Lunuganga corresponds well to the above, made up as it is of several paved or gravelled flat geometrical terraces, for human use on all sides of the house. The

LUNUGANGA

1 The approach
2 The entrance area and steps
3 The south terrace and entrance to the house
4 View towards Cinnamon Hill
5 The house
6 The north terrace
7 The guest wing and pavilion
8 The eastern terrace and galleries
9 The cliff
10 The broadwalk
11 The water gardens
12 The field of jars
13 The western terrace
14 Cinnamon Hill
15 The house on Cinnamon Hill

Source: *Geoffrey Bawa, the Complete Works*, by David Robson, Thames & Hudson 2002, p. 240. The drawing has been adapted by the author

Top:
Arriving cars have to park below and visitors are welcomed by these generous stairs leading to the house.

Bottom:
The south side of the old part of the house.

Top:
The serpentine brick wall borders the lawn of the upper north terrace like a balcony parapet. The terrace itself is characterised by the extraordinary frangipani trees, the two statues reminiscent of Michelangelo's David and by the view over the lake landscape.

Middle, left:
View of the same north terrace.

Right:
The view downhill over the water gardens, the paddy fields and the lake landscape.

Bottom:
From the south terrace the picturesque view includes the wide lawns of Cinnamon Hill.

brick serpentine wall of the grassed upper north terrace marks the shift to the serpentine park or middle ground, named the Middle Walk, at Lunuganga. The serpentine lines of the brick-kerb set out here may owe something to the undulating lines of Borromini's church balconies in Rome. Nevertheless, a play with redundant curves was also the privilege of English gentlemen. The sublime background requirement of the Picturesque as it is seen at Lunuganga is both natural and man-made. It contains great lawns, tree clumps, flat rice-fields and lily ponds, bounded by a lake, north and south.

In his book *The Gardens of Taprobane* (1937), De Mauny describes the surroundings of his island garden as reminiscent of the Italian lakes and Capri, with a touch of the South Seas. He alludes to the carved wooden columns he would add to the house, like those of the Alhambra. This is the first mention of the Alhambra, which also inspired Bawa, to appear in a Ceylonese design discourse.[5] A zone close to the araliya tree walk at Lunuganga is preempted in De Mauny's garden.[6] De Mauny wrote that had he extensive grounds at his disposal and the funds to do as he wished, he would have 'laid them out on a large scale, with wide lawns, and clumps of trees dotted about; wild in parts, formal around the house'[7] – an uncanny description of Lunuganga.

A resemblance to rolling parklands of clipped grass, dotted with clumps of trees, calling to mind the designs of Lancelot Brown, is undeniable at Lunuganga. As is the ha-ha, a road across the southern garden invisible from the house and giving the illusion of openness. The 18-century Baroque gardens at Stowe, Buckinghamshire, or Stourhead in Wiltshire are cited as sources of inspiration. Bawa did not share De Mauny's fascination with flowers, colour or his taste in garden ornament.[8]

Blue tiled pools were a part of the Persian tradition; the earliest extant is probably the Bagh e Fin dating from 1590 in Kashan city, in the province of Isfahan. Pools lined with coloured tiles are seen in many of the palaces and madrassas of 16-century Morocco, including the spectacular ruin of the El Badi palace in Marrakesh.

Morocco became a French protectorate in 1912and regained its indipendence in 1956. Colonialism fostered and facilitated the French orientalists' early 20th-century obsession with Morocco and North Africa. Jacques Majorelle was typical of French artists with orientalist proclivities. He chose to live in Marrakesh and boldly patented an intense blue colour, Majorelle blue, possibly encountered in the Atlas Mountains. It was used copiously in his garden buildings and furniture. Although Bawa never used Majorelle blue, it is possible that he visited these regions. The Majorelle Garden with its blue pools opened to the public in 1947.

Another unusual feature of the Lunuganga house is the courtyard with pool, attached to the main bedroom, also encountered in the Spanish courts at *The Brief*. The spatial sensibility of this courtyard is akin to atria of the houses of Pompeii with mosaic lined pools. The courtyards and shallow blue-tiled pools also seen in his Colombo home were signature items in a few of the early Bawa-Plesner houses. Perhaps they refer to the courts of the Alhambra.

For Brian Taylor one of the main inspirations for Lunuganga is the 16th-century *Bosco Sacro* (sacred wood) at Bomarzo, in central Italy, with its complex iconographical ensemble.[9] His observations link Lunuganga closely to the Humanist tradition. Reminiscent of the *L'allée des Jarres* in Ferdinand Bac's flowerless garden and *Les Colombières* at Menton, France, both well known to Europe's cultural elite in the 1920s and 1930s, the jars have affinities with those of Lunuganga.

Bronze nudes on the edge of the north terrace, with the water as the backdrop, may refer back to Rome where Bawa once lived, in particular to the Canopus

Left:
The western lower part of Lunuganga, The Field of Jars.

Right:
View from the eastern terrace northwards over the parapet wall with the two statues and the lake.

in Hadrian's Villa at Tivoli. Other Italian gardens such as those at Capri, Pliny's rural villas and the Pompeii frescoes that depict villas hanging off cliffs looking out over water, are also worth mentioning.

David Robson thinks that Lunuganga owes more to English gardens at Stowe, Stourhead and Italian precedent, than to King Kasapya's water garden at Sigiriya.[10] Bandaranayake proposed that Bawa's design vocabulary, in particular the way he uses water and local topography, echoes the classic traditions of Anuradhapura and Sigiriya, without singling out any specific features.[11] More recently, Robson suggested that Lunuganga was inspired in part by the 'great Sri Lankan landscapes of the classical period.'[12] His claim is supported by examples from the boulders at Polontalawa Bungalow and Bentota Beach Hotel pool.[13] For his part, Robin Jones takes the view that Bawa's garden is a site that negotiates modernity and history and belongs within a Sri Lankan tradition that interrupts the dominant modernising colonial trend. There are 'meanings implicit in the landscape of Lunuganga [...] that address wider cultural concerns'. His evidence for indigenous features is the way Bawa's landscapes fully acknowledge local topography and integrate existing features. A staircase winding round a boulder outcrop, below the north cliff at Lunuganga recalls this aspect at Sigiriya. Contra Robson, he submits that the structure of views from the north and south terraces (towards the *dagoba*) draws expanses of water into the landscape in a manner not dissimilar to Sigiriya. In doing this, 'Bawa relies on picturesque aesthetic theory developed in Europe and transferred to Asia by colonial powers.' Jones posits the Bawa landscape model as 'complex'. It defies simple categorisation within a single cultural and historical origin. Jones is unsympathetic to 'the notion of plural or alternative modernities that derive from a singular unified (and western)

The water gardens, the paddy fields and the frangipani lawn avenue, called the Broadwalk.

modernity'. Thus, Bawa's architecture and landscapes are not understood as an 'alternative modernity' that references a central modern located in Europe. Neither is his output 'specifically marked by an over-arching difference or South Asian-ness'. Rather, his work 'interrupts that totalising unifying modern by restaging it.' Jones simply allows Bawa to restage the European modern.[14]

It is probably in the sensitivity to the topography, the water and the drawing in of distant vistas – an exhilarating experience at Sigiriya and the monastery gardens at Kalu Diya Pokuna, Mihintale, Kudumbigala and innumerable other elevated *giri* monastery sites – that Lunuganga most closely approaches the expansive spatial sensibilities of Sri Lanka's ancient garden designers. Unlike the western and northern terraces whose wilderness has been tamed and grassed over, the eastern terraces, originally jungle, unmistakably reinvent the wilderness of the *giri* monasteries and Kimbulapitiya.

Water is an indispensable element of Sri Lankan gardens. At Lunuganga, the main water body is the Dedduwa lake (lagoon), visible from both the north and south of the estate. Additional pools are also present. Below the northern edge, near the lake shore, Bawa created a real water garden, using rice paddy fields, temporarily flooded, as a new garden theme. The dense planting in the areas away from the lawns produces dappled shade and bright patches of light that reproduce the chiaroscuro of the *giri* monasteries.

Bawa did pay special attention to selecting plants, especially 'the bold use of foliage, epitomised in his country house garden.'[15] Most of the planting at Lunuganga was done after 1950. The two shapely plumerias, made to interlock on the northern terrace, were trained that way. While Bevis Bawa's own garden has a variety of imported plants, in later years he preferred to design using plants found within a 10-mile radius of the site.[16] Many traditions influenced Bawa in his garden design, but it is difficult to resist the powerful sense that the magic of Kimbulapitiya and the *giri* monasteries vie with the English garden for first place.

There is no evidence that Bawa was particularly interested in indigenous plants, but he did try to retain some trees from the jungle on the east. 'The beautiful ironwood and mahogany trees positioned and shaped the Garden Room.' He was sensitive to the scent of the cannon ball tree, and noted the tall, slender and elegant arecanut palms, kumbuk and moonamal.[17]

The *Culavamsa* provides lists of plants in various royal gardens at Polonnaruwa. The Palmyra palm, mangroves, Na, banana and medicinal and scented plants adorned the *Dipauyana* Island Park, built on the bund of the massive Parakrama Samudraya *weva* outside the citadel.[18] The aesthetics of planting in such formal walled gardens is not known. We do know that there were dedicated flower gardens and orchards under royal patronage.[19]

Few people were invited to Lunuganga. It is therefore strange that Bawa records that an added 'pleasure of the garden' was to see and feel the reactions of people to the place. He chose to end the 1990 monograph on the garden with the reactions, recorded in Sinhala, of a lorry driver, delivering bricks, who once took the opportunity to walk around the garden. The translation of the driver's words given, in Sinhala script, is: 'this is a very blessed place'.[20] Bawa wanted the reader to think that the garden design resonated well with people, even though they entered the premises only as labourers or servants.

Lunuganga is a work of great complexity and beauty. Geoffrey Bawa transformed what he found on site into something truly exceptional while confronting us with a new situation where everything is developed in the context of what was already there. Bawa had, as most of his works show, a rare sense for the genius loci. And in this way, he was a part of the tradition of the monks and garden designers of earlier centuries.

A shady garden pavilion invites one to pause, and is a gooc place for the portrait sculpture of Geoffrey Bawa. The slightly worn-out columns and colours are part of Bawa's aesthetics.

The Kandalama Hotel, near Dambulla (1991-1995)

Geoffrey Bawa was entrusted with the conception and construction of many hotels on the south-western ocean beach, under palm trees, most of them with generous and beautiful gardens, among them the Bentota Beach Hotel, the Triton Hotel at Amangalla, the Lighthouse Hotel near Galle and the Blue Water Hotel at Wadduwa. But the Kandalama was the first hotel inside the country, in the northern dry zone, far from the sea, in a hilly forest and lake landscape, near the Sigiriya Rock and the other sites of the Cultural Triangle.

Bawa refused the first location the Aitken Spence Company chose for their flagship hotel. Instead, he selected a long ridge terminating in a rocky outcrop on the edge of the Kandalama tank.[21] But this location, in an immaculate cultural landscape near the ancient man-made lake, provoked a wave of protest and lengthy discussions of the controversy. Even if today the hotel is well known as one of the most environmentally friendly hotels in the world, it can also be understood as a victory of multinational capital over the protesting indigenous population, supported by monks from the Dambulla temple.[22]

The location presented a great challenge. The lake, although artificial like hundreds of reservoirs in the country, at the foot of the wooded mountains, is a landscape feature that had to be preserved as such, and yet the most prominent spot was chosen for the hotel. The rocky promontory has, however, been left untouched. The building is set halfway up and follows the topography of the cliffs. Instead of rising upwards, it unfolds into two wings with a total length of almost 1 km, remaining much lower than the rocky ridge. It is like a second façade, a curtain in front of the cliffs. The metal and glass structure is overgrown and covered with vines, climbing and drooping plants.

Unlike most large hotels, which are often pretentious and imposing, here the vegetation on the façades and roofs conceals the building in the landscape. The result is a non-dominant architecture, perfectly integrated into the existing landscape. It is literally landscape architecture at its best.

The hotel is situated halfway up an arresting, wooded rocky promontory above the ancient man-made Kandalama Lake. It unfolds in two wings following both sides of the promontory, with reception, hall, auditorium, dining rooms and bars in the centre. Its unobtrusive architecture is perfectly integrated into the natural surroundings.

Top left:
The outside terrace in front of the main hall.

Top right and bottom left:
The light blue infinity pool at a lower level.

Bottom right:
The boulder pool garden at roof level.

The way to approach the hotel is a sophisticated scenario. Coming from Dambulla, one follows a simple narrow gravel road, first running through the fields and bushes of the plain on the lake level, then climbing the foot of the boulder ridge. The hotel is not yet visible – the view emerges at the very last moment. Once having reached the reception lobby, the view opens onto the Kandalama Lake. From the cave-like lobby, one cannot really see the hotel. One has to follow the black boulder rock on the left side into a dark tunnel leading to the main hotel hall, spacious, high and luminous, opening onto an outside terrace. Here the panoramic view of the lake landscape with the infinity pool in the foreground is the final surprise.

Water is an important element of the landscaping. It appears in three different manners: the wide glittering surface of the lake, the light blue infinity pool on the lower terrace level, which seems to merge with the lake, and the upper terrace boulder pool. These two pools are indeed reminescent of the infinity boulder pools of the *giri* monasteries like Kudumbigala or Nuwaragala.

There are 'gardens' intended to be frequented and used by the hotel guests, like the infinity pool garden, the boulder pool garden on the roof level and the roof gardens, especially the one where the outdoor restaurant is located. Their design is characterised by simplicity and clear geometric lines. But the more organic green spaces at the foot of the buildings, the lawns with trees and bushes, are not meant to be visited, even if it is possible to walk around them. Their role is to serve as a green foreground. Seen from the rooms, one has the impression of being immersed in the nature. Immediately

The eastern wing. The façades and most of the roofs, all are covered by vegetation. The rooms are behind a curtain of climbing and drooping plants, which resembles a second façade in front of the cliffs, so that, seen from a distance, the building is scarcely visible.

Photocomposition by Ivan Baranowski, Zurich

In front of the rooms the metal brise-soleil structures serve as supports for the climbing plants, which are populated by birds, monkeys, giant squirrels and other wildlife.

behind the windows there are the brise-soleil structures full of climbing plants, populated by monkeys and birds. On the second ground are the lawns and trees outside the hotel; behind them the lake shore appears with fishing boats and sometimes buffalos or elephants, while the calm view of the lake and the forested mountain ridges composes the horizon.

A totally different experience is gained walking along the backside corridors leading to the rooms. These are open to the nearby forested boulder cliffs and follow them, more or less in parallel, and provide the opportunity to observe the wildlife in the trees and on the rocks. At some places the rock is so near that one can touch it, at others boulders are integrated into the corridor. The design principals of the corridors are reminders of the Sigiriya gallery behind the mirror wall. But what is really modern is the contrast between the hard-line concrete structure and the rhythm of the pillars and the natural boulder rock.

'The most enduring experience for the visitor is the sensation of a building wrapping around a forested cliff face, incorporating aerial gardens and views of lakes and mountains. Bawa knew, imagined, and appreciated the composite result of Sigiriya where architecture is inseparable from the landscape, water, paintings, horticulture, and vistas. The Kandalama design, an aggregate of many contradictory layers of thought, pays witty homage to his ancestors.'[23]

Kandalama is a reinterpretation of ancient design principles. It is a series of viewing platforms facing the horizon and the lake, a kind of artificial boulder ridge, doubling the natural one. Monks' cells in series come to to mind.

'The architecture is stark and understated, emphasizing that this is not a building to look at, but a building to look from, like a giant belvedere. The guests are marooned in a huge ocean liner with decks above and cabins below that has come to rest like Noah's Ark on some faraway mountainside.'

Laki Senanayake's Gardens

Laki Senanayake (1937-2021) was one of the most talented Sri Lankan artists of his generation. After the Royal College and the Melbourne Art School, he was employed in Geoffrey Bawa's architecture office as a draughtsman. Here he met Bevis Bawa, Ena da Silva, Donald Friend, Ulrik Plesner, Barbara Sansoni and others. He contributed to the development of the drawing style typical of the Bawa studio, giving the external spaces as much weight as the interiors and representing accurately each tree. However, the strict organisation of an architect's office was not for him. In 1964 he changed to Ena da Silva's Batik studio and from 1970 worked there as an independent artist. Besides producing amazing drawings, paintings and sculptures, he was at the same time (and this is still less known) a gifted landscape gardener.

Diyabubula (the artist's own garden)

In 1970 the artist moved out of Colombo to Diyabubula near Dambulla and began gardening. Following the example of Bevis and Geoffrey Bawa, he created his own garden in an existing plantation during a long creative process. Damming a small river flowing through his property, he shaped a series of ponds of different size and form around a group of large boulders, playing with the natural topography. At its centre, perched on the boulders, he built a house for himself. It was a wooden deck on wooden pillars, with a large thatched, vegetation-covered roof without any wall. The uncovered part of the deck was a generous terrace jutting out, between the trees, over the main pool. This totally open living room allowing him to be in a direct and sensual contact with the surrounding nature corresponded to Laki's lifestyle, dressed as always was, traditionally with naked torso and a coloured sarong. In the early morning one could sometimes hear him playing the flute, conversing with the birds. At other moments of the day, he listened at high volume to classical music floating over the water through the whole garden.

The garden can be characterised as an organic water garden whose main elements are water, trees and the central boulder massif. It is a contemporary interpretation, *en miniature*, of the Sri Lankan tradition to create artificial lakes or tanks. The different ponds on different levels are connected by a system of overflows from the one to the next. A source (*bubula*, bubbling water) from where a small stream flows, is the second provision of water. Laki's garden is an oasis of biodiversity, a paradise for the birds and an open-air exhibition space for his sculptures. At every strategic point he put one of his own artworks, creating mysterious visual relations. Following the riverbed one discovers a series of cascades, sculptures, fountains and other surprises. There was no real system of constructed ways, only small footpaths which allowed for the exploration of the garden.

Arriving at Diyabubula one stands in front of a high wall with a small porticus, like the entrance of a monastic garden. A kind of courtyard, framed on the left hand by a wall, in front of the boulder with the 'house', on the right opens onto a first pond. The surprise is perfect. Outside from the entrance is Laki's nursery, where he cultivated trees, bamboo and all kind of plants for the gardens he designed for his clients, and also the well-equipped workshop where he created his metal sculptures. Diyabubula represents a 'Gesamtkunstwerk' by a great artist and landscape architect.

In 2022, after Laki's death, the garden was converted into a small luxury hotel, which is open to the public. During Laki's lifetime the site had its very specific and highly authentic quality, alas altered by the recent transformations. The water garden is, however, preserved, and the spirit of the original project is partly still present.[24]

A visitor arriving at Diyabubula, has first to cross a kind of moat before going through the enclosure wall via a small gateway into a kind of courtyard, as in a monastery. Water is already present. Behind the courtyard, a boulder and the large roof of Laki's house on pillars are visible.

The house, built of wooden pillars on the boulder, and its enormous roof, covered by vegetation, seen from the main pond. The living and sleeping area on the first floor has no walls!

Laki seated in his favourite place on the wooden deck overlooking his water garden.

A distant sculpture draws the visitor's eye to a second pond behind the main one. The ponds are separated by the river that runs between them. Many of Laki's sculptures are placed at different viewpoints or attractive spots such that the garden became a permanent exhibition of his work. Even in the riverbed Laki placed some small cascades or other features.

The Gardens of the Sigiriya Village Hotel (the second part)

An important example of Laki's talent as a landscape gardener are the gardens of the second part of the Sigiriya Village Hotel (the 1990s). The rooms of this hotel are organised in groups or rows of small cottage houses. Along the front side of these house rows are generous common garden spaces, each one devoted to a particular theme.

Differing from the first part, designed by Bevis Bawa in the 1980s, Laki, inspired by the nearby Sigiriya Royal Garden ruins, imagined an irregular geometric water garden, structured and framed by massive brick walls. The main elements of the garden spaces are some pre-existing old trees, canal-like pools, the brick walls and the walkways leading to the houses parallel to the pools. The water in the pools, mostly dark, reflects the vegetation-covered walls and the trees, and is animated by fish and other creatures.

A particularity is that, beside the entrance, every house has its own small square pool, which collects rainwater from the roofs. The brick walls, like the walls in the Sigiriya gardens, are largely colonised by mosses or covered by ferns and bromelias. Together with the ground-cover plants, these gardens offer a fascinating botanical richness and biodiversity. They have an intimate, strong, unique atmosphere. Laki Senanayake created here a convincing modern interpretation of a Sigiriya water garden.

Following the pattern of the house rows, Laki developed an irregular, but geometric design. The characteristic elements of these gardens are the massive, high brick walls and the long, canal-like black pools, which reflect the lush vegetation. Thanks to the tropical climate, the brick walls are in large part covered by ferns and mosses, an aesthetic effect that recalls the ruins of Sigiriya. Every house has its own small pool beside the entrance to collect the rainwater that comes down from the roof.

The Boulder Garden Hotel

Clusters of large boulders are a common natural feature of Sri Lanka, and many of them have been inhabited since prehistoric times. Hidden in a forested hillside near Kalawana (south from Rathnapura) there is just such a huge boulder cluster. A businessman from that region had the idea of creating there a remote retreat hotel. He entrusted with this task to the young Sri Lankan architect Lalyn Collure (now living in Canada). Realised in the beginning of the years 2000, the result is fascinating and well worth a visit.

The entrance from the parking lot and the ascent to the reception is a true journey of discovery, climbing a flight of steps under a huge boulder, passing archways or narrow passages between boulders, through courtyard-like shady extensions with cobblestones in whose joints spring water flows. Accompanied by lush large-leaved vegetation, ferns and mosses, one passes from surprise to surprise, without seeing the final destination until one is standing in front of the reception desk.

Top left:
Coming from the parking area, this is the first staircase along a huge boulder. The front sides of the steps are painted.

Top right and bottom left:
What follows is an uphill walk through narrow boulders and luxuriant vegetation.

Bottom right:
The final stretch before reaching the reception desk.

Top
The hotel building with the rooms is situated off the main ascent, hidden under the trees.

Bottom and next page:
At the final level of the ascent is the swimming pool surrounded by a wild boulder and jungle environment. The intense blue of the clean pool is in sharp contrast to the wilderness.

Immediately the Sigiriya Boulder Gardens spring to mind. The buildings of the guest rooms are restrained, almost hidden under the trees. The ascent continues. In the upper part of the complex, at the foot of mighty boulders, one discovers the swimming pool. From its edge rises a rainforest-like backdrop, whose contrast with the crystal-clear blue water has something of the unreal about it. The highlight is the open 'dining room' under a huge overhanging boulder. On its open side, the smooth concrete floor is bordered by a mirrored water surface. The wilderness is within reach. In the evening, by candlelight, the dark boulder, lit from below, looks even more formidable. Dinner becomes a very special experience in this atmosphere, accompanied by the croaking of frogs and other jungle sounds. The integration of the subtle design interventions into the natural rock formations has been perfectly achieved. The entire complex is in keeping with the ancient Sri Lankan tradition, yet it is distinctly modern.

The haphazard experience of the Boulder Garden Hotel, nestled in a hilly mantle of trees near the village of Kalawana, provokes a surprising effect. Upon arriving at the bottom of the site, one does not expect to discover a magical building. Its access is a flight of steps, embedded between two big granite boulders and originally painted. Next comes a network of narrow pebbled passageways where water flows. They branch out, one to the reception, another to the rooms and the third to a culminating point with its revelation: a bar–restaurant under a huge overhanging natural boulder next to a polygonal man-made swimming pool. Irregularly shaped but clearly defined, it contrasts with the natural surroundings, where stillness abounds. Trees and boulders are delicately intermingled. The strong contrast between the mineral and the vegetal permeates the whole layout.

At the end of the discovery walk appears the completely surprising 'dining room' beneath a gigantic overhanging boulder with a reflecting pool.
Dinner by candlelight under this immense rock is rather special!

1 Robson 2007, 25.
2 Robson 2002, 17.
3 Bawa/ Bon/ Sansoni 2006, 11.
4 Hill 2012.
5 Talvande 1937, 252.
6 Ibid., illustrations facing 234, 236.
7 Ibid., 248.
8 Minnette De Silva spoke of the influence De Mauny's Capriesque garden had on her mother's design of the garden, at their home St George's in Kandy. (De Silva 1998, 22). Bevis wrote briefly of the meandering paths and vistas and the many varieties of tropical shade trees in De Mauny's garden: 'On the west side of the house there was a delightful terrace with a Ricket's-blue floor, which came off on one's feet… [the garden] was furnished with seats and enormous pots and ornaments of his own making but of Italian design. The result was a superb creation created by one man to his own taste'. (Bawa 1985, 58-59)
9 Taylor 1999, 15.
10 Robson 2002, 238.
11 Bandaranayake, 'Looking at Geoffrey Bawa', address at ceremony to commemorate his 84th birthday, Colombo, 2003.
12 Robson 2008, Introduction.
13 Ibid., 25.
14 Jones 2011.
15 Bandaranayake, 'Looking at Geoffrey Bawa'.
16 Dooland De Silva in conversation, July 2013.
17 Bawa/ Bon/ Sansoni 2006, 121, 169.
18 Culavamsa, 73.123.
19 Senake Bandaranayake, Gamini Jayasinghe, *The Rock and Wall Paintings of Sri Lanka* (Colombo, Lake House Bookshop, 1986), 40-42.
20 Geoffrey Bawa, Lunuganga, 219.
21 See Jayewardene-Pillai 2017, p. 190.
22 Ibid., p. 191-193.
23 Ibid., p. 214.
24 I (Klaus Holzhausen) visited Diyabubula in 2008, invited by Laki himself. At that time his house and garden were in the original state, he lived there alone, assisted by some staff, concentrated on the essential, in full harmony with the world. Everything was authentic.

Afterword

Sri Lanka has its own unique culture. Its landscape and garden tradition was initiated in the Cultural Triangle, located around the centre of the country and which has been designated a UNESCO World Heritage Site: Anuradhapura, Polonnaruwa, Sigiriya, Dambulla and Kandy.

At their best, architectures and gardens express a unity inspired by their location and geology: the country's rocky landscape and its many water sources. The island consists for the most part in big boulders of solidified magma originating in ancient volcanoes, as well as metamorphic gneiss dating back more than two billion years. Examples of this combination are beautifully revealed in the Royal Gardens of Ranmasu Uyana as well as at the impressively huge rock of Sigiriya. As for monastic gardens, they express a strong link to water and its symbolic values, where the monks perform their ritual bathing. In respect of vegetation, originally there was a great number of trees, especially a variety of fruit trees characteristic of the landscape but which has now partially disappeared.

Contrary to other cultures such as those of the French and the British, the people in Sri Lanka do not pretend to dominate Nature in order to establish their own garden design: rather, they seek to create in harmony with Nature and follow its processes. While in Europe there was a radical change of style beginning in the 18th century, from Baroque to Picturesque and Romantic, the Sri Lankan tradition avoided such pitfalls.

Compared to Japanese and Chinese gardens which often conferred specific symbolic meaning on stones, mainly inspired by Laozian philosophy, the garden designers of Sri Lanka regarded stones mostly for what they are, objects of power and resistance.

Another unique aspect of the country when compared to other cultures that follow the same religion is its very distinctive form of Buddhism. A clear example of this are the characteristic semi-spherical forms of its dagobas stupas associated to a monastery and the semi-circular Moon stones marking the entrance to the temples. The latter symbolize karma: the cycle of new birth and suffering of beings who have not yet attained Nirvana. Bevis Bawa playfully introduced this feature in his delightful *Brief Garden*, along with other objects.

From the 16th century onwards, the country was colonised by Europeans – first by the Portuguese, then by the Dutch and finally by the British – who invaded the entire island and imposed their own cultural imprint. However dramatic and condemnable, this phenomenon has enriched Sri Lankan culture in a dialectical process, creating a new synthesis.

Today, with the return of the country's traditions, a new continuum is taking shape. The gardens of Geoffrey Bawa – who brought together local traditions and Italian and English influences in his masterly Lunuganga estate – and the more recent creations of Laki Senanayake and Lalyn Collure are beautiful and enduring testimonials for this astonishing synthesis. The uniqueness of Sri Lanka's landscapes and gardens hence fully justifies a place in the world's best bookshops and libraries. There are a myriad of publications on Chinese, Japanese and European gardens, but a comprehensive book on Sri Lankan gardens had yet to appear.

Gianni Biaggi

Bibliography

Classical sources

Mahavamsa (Mv) = *Mahavamsa: The Great Chronicle of Ceylon (1912)*, transl. Wilhelm Geiger, Mabel Bode, Buddhist Cultural Centre, Dehiwala 2007
Culavamsa (Cu) = *Culavamsa: being the more recent part of the Mahavamsa*, transl. Wilhelm Geiger, Mabel Rickmers, Pali Text Society, Oxford 1992
Hamsa sandesa = *Hamsa sandesa (Author Unknown)*, transl. Edmund Jayasuriya, Central Cultural Fund, Colombo 2005
Salalihini sandesa = *Salalihini sandesa of Thotagamuve Sri Rahula thera*, transl. Edmund Jayasuriya, Central Cultural Fund, Colombo 2002
ASCAR = Archaeological Survey of Ceylon Annual Report, Government Publications Bureau, Colombo
EZ = Epigraphia Zeylanica
UCHC = University of Ceylon History of Ceylon
Abeyawardana 2004 = H.A.P. Abeyawardana, *Heritage of Kandurata: Major Natural, Cultural and Historic Sites*, Central Bank of Sri Lanka, Colombo 2004

Aldrich 2018 = Robert Aldrich, *Cultural Encounters and Homoeroticism in Sri Lanka: Sex and Serendipity*, Routledge, London 2018

Ali 2004 = Daud Ali, *Courtly Culture and Political Life in Medieval India*, Cambridge University Press, Cambridge 2004

Anjalendran 2016 = Chelvadurai Anjalendran, *The Architectural Heritage of Sri Lanka*, Talisman Publishing, Colombo 2016

Bac 2001 = Ferdinand Bac, *Livre-journal 1919*, Claire Paulhan MM, Paris 2001

Bandarage 1982 = Asoka Bandarage, 'The Establishment and Consolidation of the Plantation Economy in Sri Lanka', in *Bulletin of Concerned Asian Scholars*, vol.14, no. 3 (1982), 2-22

Bandaranayake 1974 = Senake Bandaranayake, *Sinhalese Monastic Architecture*, Brill, Leiden 1974

Bandanarayake/ Jayasinghe 1986 = Senake Bandaranayake, Gamini Jayasinghe, *The Rock and Wall Paintings of Sri Lanka*, Lake House Bookshop, Colombo 1986

Bandaranayake 1999 = Senake Bandaranayake, *Sigiriya City, Palace and Royal Gardens*, Central Cultural Fund, Colombo 1999

Bandaranayake 2007 = Senake Bandaranayake, *Architecture of the Anuradhapura Period*, Art and Archeology of Sri Lanka, Colombo 2007

Bandaranayake/ Dharmasiri 2009 = Senake Bandaranayake, Albert Dharmasiri, *Sri Lankan Painting in the 20th century*, The National Trust Sri Lanka 2009

Bandaranayake 2012 = Senake Bandaranayake, *Continuities and Transformations, studies in Sri Lankan archaeology and history*, SSA Social Scientists Association, Colombo 2012

Basnayake 1983 = H. T. Basnayake, 'Early Buddhist Monasteries', in *Samskrti* 13 (3, July, Sept. 1983), 51-61

Basnayake/Hettige 2007 = H. T. Basnayake, Uda Hettige, *Polonnaruwa Civilization of Sri Lanka*, Godage, Colombo 2007

Biedermann 2014 = Zoltán Biedermann, *The Portuguese in Sri Lanka and South India: Studies in the History of Diplomacy, Empire and Trade, 1500-1650*, Harrassowitz, Wiesbaden 2014

Bawa 1985 = Bevis Bawa, *Briefly by Bevis,* Sapumal Foundation, Colombo 1985

Bawa/ Bon/ Sansoni 2006 = Geoffrey Bawa, Christoph Bon, Dominic Sansoni, *Lunuganga*, Marshall Cavendish Editions, Singapore 2006

Brohier 2000 = Richard Leslie Brohier, *Seeing Ceylon*, Sooriya Publishers, 4th ed., Colombo 2000

Burrows 1899 = Stephen Montagu Burrows, *Buried Cities of Ceylon: A Guide Book to Anuradhapura and Polonaruwa*, A. M. and J. Ferguson, Colombo 1899

Carrithers 1983 = Michael Carrithers, *The Forest Monks of Sri Lanka: An Anthropological and Historical Study*, Oxford University Press, Oxford 1983

Cave 1921 = Henry William Cave, *Colombo*, Pearson, Colombo 1921

Chandawimala 2016 = Rangama Chandawimala, *Heterodox Buddhism: The School of Abhayagiri*, Colombo 2016

Collins 1998 = Steven Collins, *Nirvana and Other Buddhist Felicities*, Cambridge University Press, Cambridge 1998

Cramer 2001 = L. H. Cramer, *Journal* of the National *Science* Foundation of *Sri Lanka (Bio.)* 28 (2001), 21-33

Cooray 2012 = Cooray Nilan, *The Sigiriya Royal gardens: Analysis of the landscape architectonic composition*, CreateSpace, s.l. 2012

De Groot 2006 = Veronique De Groot, 'The archaeological remains of the Ratu Boko: from Sri Lankan Buddhism to Hinduism', in *Indonesia and the Malay World* 34 (2006), 55-74

De Silva 1996 = Nimal De Silva, *Landscape Tradition of Sri Lanka: Philosophy, Principles and Practices*, Devco Designers and Publishers, Colombo 1996

De Silva/ Beumer 1988 = R. K. de Silva and W. G. M. Beumer, *Illustrations and Views of Dutch Ceylon 1602-1796*, E. J. Brill, Leiden 1988

De Silva 1998 = Minnette de Silva, *The Life and Work of an Asian Woman Architect*, Smart Media, Colombo 1998

De Silva 2023 = Shayari de Silva, Geoffrey Bawa, *Drawing from the Archives*, Lars Müller, Zurich 2023

Deraniyagala 2007 = S. U. Deraniyagala, 'The Prehistory and Protohistory of Sri Lanka', in Leelananda Prematilleke, Senake Bandaranayake., S. U. Deraniyagala, Roland Silva (eds), *The Art and Archaeology of Sri Lanka*, 1, Central Cultural Fund, Colombo 2007, 1-96

J. B. Dissanayake, *Water Culture: The Sri Lankan Heritrage*, Ministry of Environment and Parliamentary Affairs, Colombo 1992

Dissanayake 1987 = J.B. Dissanayake, *Mihintale, Cradle of Sinhala Buddhist Civilisation*, Lake House Investments Ltd Colombo 1987

Brent Elliott, *Victorian Gardens,* Timber Press, Portland, Oregon, 1986

Godakumbura 1955 = Charles Godakumbura, *Sinhalese Literature*, Colombo Apothecaries' Company, Colombo 1955, 183-207

Goonetilleke 2012 = Janaka Goonetilleke et al. (eds.), *Atapattu Walawwa*, Galle 2012

Gunawardana 1989 = R.A.L.H. (Leslie) Gunawardana, 'Anuradhapura: ritual, power and resistance in a precolonial South Asian city', in Daniel Miller, Michael Rowlands, Christopher Tilley (eds), *Domination and Resistance*, Taylor and Francis, London 1989, 155-210

Herbert 2011 = Eugenia W. Herbert, « *Flora's Empire* », University of Pennsylvania Press, 2011

Haeckel 1883 = Ernest Haeckel, *A Visit to Ceylon and India,* Kegan, Trench and Co, London 1883

Haeckel 2008 = 'Art forms in nature: the prints of Ernst Haeckel', a reprint in English by Prestel, 2008

Hill 2012 = Rosemary Hill, 'As God Intended', review of Jane Brown, *The Omnipotent Magician*, *London Review of Books*, 34, (1, 5 January 2012), 18-20

Hobhouse 2003 = Penelope Hobhouse, *Gardens of Persia*, Cassell Illustrated, London 2003

Hocart 1924 = A. M. Hocart, *Memoirs of the Archaeological Survey of Ceylon*, vol. 1, Ceylon Archaeological Department, Colombo 1924

Higuchi 1988 = Tadakiko Higuchi, *The visual and spatial structure of Landscapes*, MIT Press, Cambridge Mass. 1988

Jayewardene-Pillai 2007 = Shanti Jayewardene-Pillai, *Imperial Conversations: Indo-Britons and the Architecture of South India,* New Dehli, Yoda Press, New Dehli 2007

Jayewardene-Pillai 2017 = Shanti Jayewardene-Pillai, *Geoffrey Manning Bawa: Decolonizing Archietcture*, National Trust Sri Lanka, Colombo 2017

Jones 2011 = Robin Jones, 'Memory, modernity and history: the landscapes of Geoffrey Bawa in Sri Lanka, 1948-1998', in *Contemporary South Asia*, 19,1 (March 2011) 9-24

Jekyll/ Hussey 1918 = Gertrude Jekyll, Christopher Hussey, *Garden Ornament*, Country Life, London 1918

Jekyll 1913 = Gertrude Jekyll, *Gardens for Small Country Houses,* Country Life, London 1913

Jekyll 1908 = Gertrude Jekyll, *Color in the Flower Garden,* Country life, London 1908

Jordan/ Wessing 1996 = R. E. Jordan, R. Wessing, 'Human Sacrifice at Prambanan', in KITLV journals, *Bijdragen tot de Taal-, Land- en Volkenkunde*, 152 (1996), 45-73

Lewcock 2014 = Ronald Lewcock, 2014, 31

McAlpine/ Robson 1983 = W. R. McAlpine, David Robson, *Ritigala*, Central Cultural Fund, Colombo 1983

Moldrich 2016 = Donovan Moldrich, *Bitter Berry Bondage: the Nineteeth Century Coffee Workers of Sri Lanka*, 2nd edition, Neptune Publications, Colombo 2016, 7

Moonesinghe 2017 = Vinod Moonesinghe *From Cinnamon Forests to Cinnamon Gardens*, Roar Reports, retrieved 2 April 2017

Mori 1999 = Sodō Mori, *Mahayana Buddhism in Sri Lanka*, ARM Corp., Nagoya 1999

Mudiyanse 1967 = Nandasena Mudiyanse, *Mahayana monuments in Ceylon,* M. D. Gunasena and Co. Ltd., Colombo 1967

Nikaya Samgraha, by D. M. de Z. Wickremasinghe, Colombo 1908

Nitschke 1991 = Gunter Nitschke, *The Architecture of the Japanese Garden*, Taschen, Oldenberg 1991

Ottewill 1989 = David Ottewill, *The Edwardian Garden,* Yale University Press, New Haven 1989

Paranavitana 1954 = Senarat Paranavitana, Art *and Architecture of Ceylon: Polonnaruwa Period*, Arts Council of Ceylon, Colombo 1954

Peebles 2001 = Patrick Peebles, *The Plantation Tamils of Ceylon,* Leicester University Press, New-York 2001

Pethiyagoda 2007 = Rohan Pethiyagoda, *Pearls, Spices and Green Gold, an illustrated History of Biodiversity Exploration in Sri Lanka*, WHT Publications, Colombo 2007

Prematilleke/ Silva 1968 = Leelananda Prematilleke, Roland Silva, 'A Buddhist Monastic Type of Ancient Ceylon showing Mahayanist Influence', in *Artibus Asiae*, vol. XXX, Ascona 1968, 61-84

Prematilleke/ Silva 1989 = Leelananda Prematilleke, Roland Silva, 'A Buddhist monastic complex of the medieval period in Sri Lanka', in Daniel Miller, Michael Rowlands, Chris Tilley (eds), *Domination and Resistance*, Routledge, London 1989, 196-210

Prematilleke 2007 = Leelananda Prematilleke, 'The Architecture of Polonnaruwa and Other Contemporary Sites', in Leelananda Prematilleke, Senake Bandaranayake., S. U. Deraniyagala, Roland Silva (eds), *The Art and Archaeology of Sri Lanka*, 1, Central Cultural Fund, Colombo 2007, 295-360

Priyanka 2010 = Benille Priyanka, *Deciphered Records from the Mirror Wall at Sigiriya*, Godage International Publishers, Colombo 2010

Rahula 1966 = Walpola Rahula, *History of Buddhism in Ceylon,* MD Gunasena, Colombo 1966

Robinson 1994 = William Robinson, *The Wild Garden,* Sagapress/Timber Press, Portland, Oregon, 1994

Robson 2002 = David Robson, *Geoffrey Bawa*, Thames & Hudson, London 2002

Robson 2007 = David Robson, *Beyond Bawa: modern masterworks of monsoon Asia*, Thames and Hudson, London 2007

Robson 2008 = David Robson, *Bawa, the Sri Lanka Gardens,* Thames&Hudson, London 2008

Robson/ Daswatte 2011 = David Robson and Channa Daswatte, *Geoffrey Bawa 1919-2003*, Geoffrey Bawa Trust, Colombo 2011

Schopen 2006 = Gregory Schopen, 'The Buddhist Monastery and the Indian Garden: Aesthetics, assimilation, and the siting of monastic establishments', in *Journal of the American Oriental Society*, 126, 4 (2006), 487-505

Seneviratna 1983 = Anuradha Seneviratna, *Kandy, an illustrated survey*, Central Cultural Fund, Colombo 1983

Seymour = A.D.D. Seymour, « *Ward, Henry George* », Oxford Dictionary of National Biography

Sharma 2009 = Jyoti P. Sharma, 'The Mughal gardens of the Indian Sub-continent and the colonial legacy: the treatment of Delhi's Shalamar Bagh', *Journal of Landscape Architecture*, 2 (Autumn 2009), 32-47

Silva 2007 = Roland Silva, 'Architecture of the Thupa, Bodhimanda, Uposathaghara and Patimaghara', in *AASL,* 2007, 463-526

Strickland 2011 = Keir M. Strickland, *The Jungle Tide: 'Collapse' in Early Mediaeval Sri Lanka*, Ph.D, Durham University

Sundberg 2004 = Jeffrey Roger Sundberg, 'The wilderness monks of the Abhayagirivihare and the origins of Sino-Javanese esoteric Buddhism', *KITLV* Journals *Bijdragen tot de Taal-, Land-en Volkenkunde* 160 (1), Leiden 2004, 95-123

Sundberg 2016 = Jeffrey Roger Sundberg, 'Mid-9th Century Adversity for Sinhalese Esoteric Buddhist Exemplars in Java', in Acri, Andrea (ed.), *Esoteric Buddhism in Medieval Maritime Asia: Networks of Masters, Texts, Icons*, Singapore, Yusof Ishak Institute, London 2016, 349-379

Talvande 1921 = Maurice Talvande, Count de Mauny-Talvande, *Gardening in Ceylon*, Colombo 1921

Talvande 1937 = Maurice Talvande, Count de Mauny-Talvande, *The Gardens of Taprobane,* Williams and Norgate, London 1937

Tankard 2004 = Judith B. Tankard, *Gardens of the Arts and Crafts Movement,* Harry N. Abrams Inc., État de New York 2004

Taylor 1999 = Brian Brace Taylor, *Geoffrey Bawa*, Thames&Hudson, London 1999

Tennent 1859 = James Emerson Tennent, *Ceylon: An Account of the Island Physical, Historical and Topographical*, Longman, Green, Longman, and Roberts, London 1859

Von Schroeder 1990 = Ulrich Von Schroeder, *Buddhist Sculptures of Sri Lanka*, Visual Dharma Publications, Hong Kong 1990

Wijesuriya 1998 = Gamini Wijesuriya, *Buddhist Meditation Monasteries of Ancient Sri Lanka*, Dept. of Archaeology, Colombo 1998

Glossary

Arama	Residence of monks
Ath	Elephant
Bodhi tree	Walls framing a Bodhi tree, or a roofed structure around the tree, which is the subject of devotion
Boulder	Big stone, name for Sri Lanka's typical rounded Gneiss rock formations with many natural caves
Cancamana	Path for walking meditation in monasteries or in front of hermit caves
Chunam plaster	Layer of lime (calcium carbonate)
Diguvil	Long pond of water
Gala	Stone, rock
Gal-ge	Cave
Gewatta	Compound of a house
Giri	Hill
Kanda	Mountain
Kema pool	Part man-made rock pool for water storage for man and animals, also used for Buddhist rituals, some with panoramic view
Mahavamsa / Culavamsa	Ancient written chronologies of Srilankan Kings
Mahavihara	Great Monastery, high residential university for Buddhist monks at Anuradhapura
Naga	Cobra, also name of ancient tribes in South Asia
Pancayatana	Five unit geometrical lay-out of ritual and domestic buildings in Buddhist monasteries
Parivena	Educational institute for Buddhist monks
Pokuna	Pond
Puncalasa	Ornamented pot used for decoration signifying prosperity
Sangha	Monastic assembly, organization or institution of Buddhist monks
Stupa / Dagoba	A relic burial mound, or a mound-like hemispheric structure containing relics
Tank / Wewa	Man-made lake for water storage for irrigation
Thera	Monk
Theravada, Mahayana and Vajrayana	The 3 major branches or schools of Buddhism
Uyana	Garden
Vihara	Temple
Walawwa (valavva)	House or residence of an aristocratic person

Credits

All photographs, if not otherwise stated,
were taken by Klaus Holzhausen.

All aerial photographs from a helicopter
were taken by Olivier Lasserre in February 2010.

All surveys, drawings or revision of existing plans
are the work of Klaus Holzhausen and Charlotte Thietart.

Silvana Editoriale

Chief Executive
Michele Pizzi

Editorial Director
Sergio Di Stefano

Art Director
Giacomo Merli

Editorial Coordinator
Émilie Hanmer

Copy Editing
Mariangela Palazzi-Williams

Layout
Diego Mantica

Production Coordinator
Antonio Micelli

Editorial Assistant
Giulia Mercanti

Photo Editor
Silvia Sala

Press Office
Alessandra Olivari, press@silvanaeditoriale.it

ISBN 978-88-366-5955-5

Silvana Editoriale S.p.A.
via dei Lavoratori, 78
20092 Cinisello Balsamo, Milano
tel. 02 453 951 01
www.silvanaeditoriale.it

Reproductions, printing and binding in Italy
Printed by Tecnostampa Pigini Group Printing Division,
Loreto - Trevi
Printed in December 2024

FSC www.fsc.org MIX Paper | Supporting responsible forestry FSC® C127663